Breakthrough!

BREAK! THROUGH

90 PROVEN STRATEGIES TO OVERCOME CREATIVE BLOCK & SPARK YOUR IMAGINATION

ALEX CORNELL, EDITOR

With a foreword by Erik Spiekermann

PRINCETON ARCHITECTURAL PRESS, NEW YORK

Contents

When a bricklayer doesn't feel like adding yet another brick to the wall or when a cobbler is bored with driving nails into leather, does anybody take notice? Are there consequences outside of the wall being a little crooked or the shoe glued instead of nailed? Probably not, as these are choices that come with the job. Just like a surgeon cannot be averse to the sight of blood and a baker cannot work if allergic to flour, all trades carry certain conditions that should be known to those who choose to practice them.

Why, then, do we creatives get special consideration? Creative block is a known and expected obstacle—one that all suffer from and most complain about. Why is braving it almost a requirement for being considered truly creative? Surely, there must be techniques for overcoming the occasional resentment surrounding having to conjure up one more idea, write another sentence, invent a funny line.

Whenever I complain to my mother about the predicament of being totally stuck for inspiration, feeling almost brain dead, and wondering why I ever got into the business of designing things that had to appear fresh, witty, and even beautiful, she would tell me to shut up and stop making excuses for the only thing she thought wrong: in her eyes, I was just being lazy.

She may have a point. Procrastination is certainly one of the most common symptoms of creative block. And for some of us, it is even a technique to get the intellectual engine restarted.

In this book Alex Cornell has collected the solutions and strategies of a diverse range of creative people on how they deal with inspiration ruts. Like me, you can take solace in the knowledge that you are not alone in this struggle. The one thing we all have in common is the awareness that—however bad it may seem—we always get over it, eventually.

This project began in 2010 when I e-mailed my friend Scott Hansen with the idea for a blog post on creative block for his website ISO50. I figured I'd write a piece about it, maybe even propose a strategy or two, and our readers would be forever cured of this ailment. Of course, I got no further than a few paragraphs before I was struck with my own bout of block. How cliché! I gave up and snapped my pencil (which these days means relieving my keyboard of its batteries).

I soldiered on. Sending out SOS e-mails to friends and artists I admired, I asked them for help. "Send me your wisdom!" I cried. Twenty-five wrote back, and we published their strategies in a small blog post. It was and continues to be our most popular post ever. Clearly, I wasn't the only one who was periodically struck by the murky wave of creative nothingness.

The topic continued to fascinate me, not so much because I enjoyed it, but because it presented itself so inconveniently often. Another project, another block. I decided further action was necessary. While the blog post was a worthy potshot at creative block, we needed something more substantial, something more robust and with more firepower. A book, yes! That would do. Books are more substantial (physically heavier!) and require the readers to detach themselves from their computers (most likely the tool for all procrastination and the source of all block anyway).

Two years and an unfathomable number of e-mails later, the book exists.

I think I can safely assume that you have, at one point in your career, been enveloped by a block of some kind. It's refreshing to remember once in a while that creative block happens to everyone. To make us all feel better, I asked ninety terribly inspiring creative people for their strategies—not just so we can learn from them but also to trick them into tacitly acknowledging their own susceptibility to this condition. You'll find their wisdom and their tactics in this book for your immediate implementation.

When I imagine the people in this book working, I don't picture blank pieces of paper and broken pencils. I don't picture empty screens, endless cups of coffee, or late nights. I picture ideas branching out from everywhere, ripe for the taking. As you'll find out, this is not the case. We are creative people, and with creativity comes the occasional (or frequent) block. For those few contributors who wrote back to me with the response "I don't get creative block," let it be publicly known that I don't believe you! Either that or I'm jealous.

In this book you'll find strategies of all sorts, and since one block is not the same as the next, a diverse array of methods is necessary to have at your disposal. This book is that array, the start of your arsenal. Pick it up in times of need, read it from cover to cover, a page here and there, whatever. It's meant to be versatile, and it's meant to help.

———

Oh, and I should also mention my own strategy for overcoming creative block: Random Task Assignment (RTA). It's like spontaneous word association but with tasks. Let's try it:

1. **Destroy your computer**—either on purpose or by accident. (I typically take the accident approach, but I'm sure destroying it on purpose might be exciting.) If you have a nemesis of some sort, it might help to get them involved. Danger and intrigue!

2. **Find a way to procure a large weather balloon and several exotic plants.** Without your computer this may be difficult. A challenge!

3. **Throw a good-bye party for the weather balloon** (and its cargo) in an abandoned warehouse and invite all of your town's citizens to attend.

4. **Release the weather balloon, and say goodbye.** Continue on this path of random task assignment until you're either arrested or think of something better to do. Of course, if you do the latter, you'll have succeeded in your quest to overcome your block.

That's how I do it anyway. Read on to learn from the heavy hitters.

They say an elephant never forgets. Well, you are not an elephant. Take notes, constantly. Save interesting thoughts, quotations, films, technologies…the medium doesn't matter, so long as it inspires you. When you're stumped, go to your notes like a wizard to his spellbook. Mash those thoughts together. Extend them in every direction until they meet.

Your notebook is feeling thin? Then seek assistance and find yourself a genius. Geniuses come in many shapes and colors, and they often run in packs. If you can find one, it may lead you to others. Collaborate with geniuses. Send them your spells. Look carefully at theirs. What could you do together? Combination is creation.

Beware of addictive medicines. Everything in moderation. This applies particularly to the Internet and your sofa. The physical world is ultimately the source of all inspiration. Which is to say, if all else falls: take a bike ride.

FIND YOURSELF A

GENIUS

I have always found that there is an implication that writer's block is some odd obstacle on the otherwise smooth road of creation. As far as my own work goes, I have to say that my entire creative process is one big and viciously tough writer's block. Ideas never come easily to me, and the desperation that comes with staring at a white piece of paper, being anxious about having finally run out of ideas for good, is simply my everyday work routine. The only remedy I know of is to keep trying, drawing, banging my head against the table. Walks in the park, chats with friends, going to a museum are good fun, but when I am struggling with a creative problem, I find they are just ways of procrastinating.

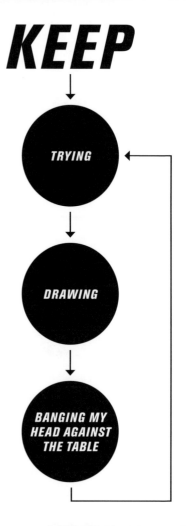

Maybe it just takes

showing up.

Cheers. Whatcha gonna do with a blocked toilet? I mean that's all it is, right? A bung that needs pulling to let the clear waters of inspiration flow.

Maybe. Or maybe it just takes showing up. Going back again and again to write or paint or sing or cook.

Some days the genius will be in you, and you will sail. Other days the lead will line the slippers, and you'll be staring into the void of your so-called creative mind, feeling like a fraud. It's all part of the big ole cycle of creativity, and it's a healthy cycle at that.

The ego bobbing up. And down on the sea of turning up!

Just keep going, and let go of the wheel. The good stuff will sometimes flow when you're least expecting it. The artist's job really does seem to be catching those ghosts as they fly out of the soul.

The solution to a problem:

- ☐ Slice and chop two medium onions into small pieces.
- ☐ Put a medium-sized pan on medium heat with a few drops of olive oil.
- ☐ Add the onions to the pan, with a pinch of salt and pepper.
- ☐ Chop finely a variety of fresh chilies (bird's eye, Scotch bonnet, green, and red).
- ☐ Add the chilies to the pan, stir together, and cook for eight minutes.
- ☐ Add about 500 g of extra-lean beef mince into the pan.
- ☐ Stir in so that the beef is coated and lightly browned (should take approximately two minutes).
- ☐ Add salt and pepper.
- ☐ Add red kidney beans and tinned chopped tomatoes.
- ☐ Stir well.
- ☐ Add a pinch of cinnamon.
- ☐ Cook on low heat for approximately twenty minutes.
- ☐ Measure a cup and a half of basmati rice into a medium-sized pan.
- ☐ Add two-and-a-quarter cups (the same cup you measured the rice in) of cold water to the pan with the rice.
- ☐ Boil on high heat until the lid rattles.
- ☐ Turn down to low heat and cook for eight minutes.
- ☐ After eight minutes turn the heat off the rice and leave for four minutes (with the lid on).

- ☐ Plate up the rice (on the side), add the chili.
- ☐ Pour a large glass of red wine (preferably from Australia or New Zealand).

Now the important problem-solving part:

- ☐ Take the dirty plates and pans to the sink.
- ☐ Run a mixture of hot (not too hot) and cold water.
- ☐ Add a smidgen of washing-up liquid (preferably for sensitive skin).
- ☐ Start washing up; the mundane kicks in.
- ☐ The mind clears, and new thoughts and ideas appear.
- ☐ Enjoy a second glass of wine to savor the moment.

Weird printing techniques, faded colors, antiquated design decisions, old photos, fonts that have fallen into obscurity.

When I get creative block, I look through my own personal archive for a while. I have several thousand images I've collected over time, all old, the newest being from the 1970s. There is something about looking at ephemeral imagery from the past—especially things that nobody else may ever see again—that I find very compelling. Weird printing techniques, faded colors, antiquated design decisions, old photos, fonts that have fallen into obscurity. I will look at a faded color photo from the 1970s or one of those colored-in Victorian postcards or a cookbook for making fifty instant meals and get really excited to work—to manipulate some element of all this forgotten printed matter into something new that I will make. To bring it back in my own way. What can I say? I guess I'm pretty nostalgic.

Ideas often happen one of two ways: recalling reference material from my blurry memory or exploiting something from our home or assorted collections as a jump-off. In some cases, an image of the completed piece pops into my head as the project is being discussed. I usually come to the conclusion that the image in my head sucks and begin sketching and sniffing around the objects that have caught my eye over the years. All these things marinate in a hearty blend of indecision until the real problem solver is turned on: my hot water heater. Yes, I credit my hot water heater for supplying an almost constant flow of warm clarity that showers creative blocks down the drain.

A HEARTY BLEND OF

INDE CISION

If the remedy was exact, I'd patent it, design the packaging, and make some money.

Ah, the block. Enemy of my creativity.

After many encounters, I eventually realized that when the block hits, I just need to calm down and try to restart my mind. A reboot, so to speak. Not sure why, but I get in this crazed mind-set, tearing through undeveloped ideas, convincing myself that none are good enough to finish. Needless to say, I make no progress. At all. Nada. And when I'm in this headspace, its all a downward spiral unless I do something about it. Fast.

First and foremost, I get up and walk away. Deadline or not. If it's not happening, it's not going to happen. After I walk away from my work, there's no exact science to what I do. But for this topic's sake, it usually resembles something like this: I migrate into the kitchen, leaving the blocked headspace and crap work behind me. Before I do anything else, I pour myself a glass of wine. I find a new room, with a new place to sit for a while. And I pray. The act of closing my eyes and talking quietly, alone, always gives me an unparalleled peace. I really can't explain or do it justice with words.

I'll follow that up with music. Something instrumental. For instance, one of Ennio Morricone's *In Lounge* albums or a Steven Soderbergh film score composed by David Holmes. Both composers are absolutely brilliant. I've always loved this type of music. It inspires me more than most. I sit and listen and allow my mind to be informed by a different art form. Most of my inspiration comes from things I don't already know. This incredible music just feels like design for the ears. It never fails to paint a new picture in my head. Not having lyrics telling me what to think is refreshing. By that point I'm usually inspired enough to pull out a pad and sketch. Sketching usually leads to solid ideas, and solid ideas bring me back into my workspace—with a renewed mind.

When all is said and done, the process may take thirty minutes or it may take a day. If the remedy was exact, I'd patent it, design the packaging, and make some money. But it isn't. So I won't.

Salut.

An intern who once worked for me started every design project in a state of creative paralysis, brought on by the seemingly infinite visual possibilities at his disposal. He went around in circles for days, the carousel of possibility never stopping. I did my best to explain to him that he didn't have a direction yet because he hadn't framed the problem, that he didn't have any idea what he wanted to communicate.

One of the best ways to avoid creative block is to take the problem that's handed to you and redefine it in a way you find compelling, intriguing, or exciting. One way to do that is to consider the assignment from a completely different angle: How would the

WHAT IF

WINSTON

CHURCHILL

WAS DESIGNING THIS PACKAGING

???

solution differ if the product was for dogs rather than humans? How would we communicate then? What if the restaurant was themed around a movie? What if Winston Churchill was designing this packaging? How would that work? What if the goal wasn't to sell these, but to promote an event?

Changing your perspective and considering a different viewpoint can result in unique and unexpected solutions, and there are a million ways to do it. I have sketchbook after sketchbook of cataloged ideas and "wrong" solutions from past projects. I usually break blocks by leafing through those. Although I rarely find the solution, it helps me consider the problem from different, unexpected angles. That's extremely valuable.

My other trick for getting past a creative block is giving up. Usually, conceptualizing a design project goes one of two ways: either something hits me like a ton of bricks during conversations with the client, or I go through the entire brand exercise with no epiphany. When that happens, I spend a period of intense immersion, where I absorb everything I can about the client. I look through their history, culture, and milestones, and I think about them almost constantly. Then I give up.

By give up, I mean that I stop actively working on the project. I stop thinking about it, I stop stressing about it, and I ignore it completely. I go for a bike ride or a long walk, I get a beer with friends, or I go see a movie. A day or two later when the project is completely out of my mind, the ton of bricks lands.

For any of this to happen, you have to have a firm grasp of what you want to communicate, and a solid framework defining your goals. Otherwise you never get off the carousel.

Creative block affects me just like anyone else. I never know when one will strike or when it will be cured. The best way to overcome any creative block is to make a lot of mistakes. The more mistakes you make, the more you learn, the more you grow, and the more you evolve as an artist and person. It's through making mistakes that I discover new ideas in my workflow.

One of my absolute favorite ways to kick creative block to the curb is to pack up my car, point to a spot on a map, and drive there. The last time I did that, I ended up in the Mojave Desert and climbed the third largest dune in the United States on a Monday afternoon in the spring, with the entire Kelso Dunes to myself. If I can't travel, I'll watch the local radar or traffic on TV stations at 4 a.m. There's something about maps, radars, and the static of the AM radio that excites me.

Often when I drive, I'll listen to AM radio along the way. I try to find informational stations to listen to. On my way to the Mojave Desert, I tuned into the AM station in Barstow, California, that provides listeners with Mojave Desert travel information. When I'm at home in Los Angeles, I listen to 530 AM, which is the LAX airport terminal-information station. Listening to these mundane stations puts me at ease, and I get lost daydreaming about traveling.

MAKE A LOT OF MISTAKES

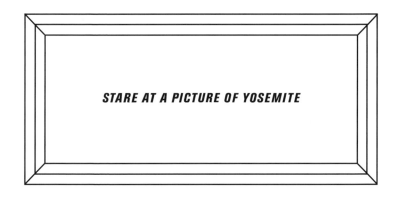

STARE AT A PICTURE OF YOSEMITE

I live in New York City, but secretly I'm a nature guy. So when I'm stuck in a creative rut, I often want to escape my surroundings to find a more inspiring place to think or work. If I'm in my apartment, then I sometimes go outside for a walk. If I'm at my desk at work, then I go lie down on the couch and close my eyes. If I'm really in a bad place, and I really can't shake it, then I've been known to drive hundreds of miles to Vermont or Maine just to envelop myself with glorious natural surroundings. I've come up with my best, most creative ideas driving around by myself in silence.

Changing my location literally helps me get out of the negative or unproductive space I sometimes find myself in. My most creative moments occur when I can immerse myself in the outdoors and get lost in its beauty. Escaping to someplace beautiful isn't always possible, especially in a city, but changing your surroundings usually is. Get away, go outside, even just stare at a picture of Yosemite—who knows, it just might help.

If you're reading this, it's safe to assume that you're a creative person. Sometimes we all just need to be reminded of that. It sounds a bit existential and wishy-washy, but it's easy to undercut ourselves and forget how talented and imaginative we are as artists and designers. I find putting yourself in workhorse mode— simply just keeping at it until you strike your own gold—can be the most rewarding way out of a creative rut. There have been times when I've just sat there doing something over and over in different ways, scrapping every idea in frustration, until I finally made that one right pencil stroke, took that one photo with the right angle, chose a slightly different shade of the same color— until finally everything comes together absolutely perfectly, effectively giving a big, fat middle finger to the rut behind you.

KEEP AT IT UNTIL YOU STRIKE YOUR OWN GOLD

Somehow things always work out in the end.

When I experience creative block, I do a few different things:

☐ **Take long showers.** Somehow, I can think a little differently while I'm in the shower. It washes away my old thoughts, and I feel renewed.

☐ **Clean my surroundings.** I cannot think clearly when there's a mess around me.

☐ **If these haven't worked, I go for a bike ride,** and I try not to think about the project at all. Somehow things always work out in the end.

Reading List:

☐ William Green. *The Observer's Book of Aircraft*. London: F. Warne & Co., 1972.

☐ Robert Carleton Hobbs. *Mark Lombardi: Global Networks*. New York: Independent Curators International, 2003.

☐ Rudolf Hostettler. *The Printer's Terms: Termes techniques des industries graphiques*. London: A. Redman, 1949.

☐ Martin Kippenberger. *Martin Kippenberger: Die gesamten Plakate 1977–1997*. Cologne: Buchhandlung Walther König, 1998.

☐ Neil F. Michelsen. *The American Book of Tables: Placidus Tables of Houses, Time Tables, Interpolation Tables, How to Cast a Natal Horoscope*. San Diego: ACS Publications, 1984.

☐ Harold A. Murtz, ed. *The Gun Digest Book of Exploded Firearms Drawings*. Northfield, IL: DBI Books, 1982.

☐ John L. Nanovic. *Secret Writing: An Introduction to Cryptograms, Ciphers, and Codes*. New York: Dover Publications, 1974.

☐ Erwin Raisz. *General Cartography*. New York: McGraw-Hill, 1948.

☐ Wolfgang Richter. *Rekorde, Einmaligkeiten, Kuriositäten in der DDR*. Berlin: Verlag Neues Deutschland, 1987.

☐ Robert F. Scott, ed. *Shooter's Bible*. 70th edition. New York: Stoeger, 1978.

☐ Taryn Simon. *An American Index of the Hidden and Unfamiliar*. London: Steidl, 2007.

- [ ] A. Stork. *MM, Didot, Pica, Inch: Umrechnungstabellen für das Druckgewerbe*. Zutphen: Edition Terra, 1980.

- [ ] Jan Tschichold. *Die neue Typographie: ein Handbuch für zeitgemäss Schaffende* [*Jan Tschichold: A Life in Typography*]. Berlin: Bildungsverband der deutschen Buchdrucker, 1928.

- [ ] Eliot Wigginton. *Foxfire 2: Ghost Stories, Spring Wild Plant Foods, Spinning and Weaving, Midwifing, Burial Customs, Corn Shuckin's, Wagon Making, and More Affairs of Plain Living*. Garden City, NY: Anchor Books, 1973.

- [ ] ———. *Foxfire 4: Fiddle Making, Springhouses, Horse Trading, Sassafras Tea, Berry Buckets, Gardening, and Further Affairs of Plain Living*. Garden City, NY: Anchor Books, 1977.

- [ ] Victor Zimmermann. *Praktische Winke für den Umgang mit Satz und Schrift*. Frankfurt: D. Stempel AG, 1962.

HAVE YOUR HEART

BROKEN

Here's my advice (pick any two or three):

☐ **Hitchhike to Mexico.** Stop in the capital for lunch. Ride the metro if you want to see a little bit of the city. (The Anthropology Museum is great.) Then catch a bus south. Any town, doesn't matter. If you have to rely on the Internet, go back to El Paso and start over. One way or another, get to a small town on the coast. Find a place with tables by the beach, order something to eat, sit, and listen to the ocean. The point of all this is shrimp with cayenne pepper and lime, rough corn tortillas, grilled squid, if they have it. As you eat, remember that when you woke up this morning, you had no idea this place was here. When it gets late, buy some mezcal at the stand next to the restaurant. There'll be a girl there doing her homework in a small notebook. Remember to save the bottle, which is clear glass and has a homemade label. Share drinks with everyone, have some beer, eventually head over to the hotel, which also faces the surf. Get a good night's rest. Tomorrow you've got to get back to work.

☐ **Have your heart broken.** It worked for Rei Kawakubo. You'll realize the work you'd been doing wasn't anywhere near your potential.

☐ **Read "Instructions: Early Epiphanies" by Elizabeth Macklin** (#1 above is basically stolen from this poem) or, if you can find it, "The Cure Cure" by Sally Eckhoff. Do not mistake these as being about food—that's incidental. The details are what matter. There's also that Raymond Carver poem with the cigarette stubbed out in a jar of mustard. And the story in James Joyce's *Dubliners* with the strange line about what a woman **→**

standing in shadow listening to distant music is a symbol of. Writers are the most acute and judicious observers—far better than graphic designers or painters. (And don't even bother with architects.)

☐ **Read old J. Peterman catalogs.** I'm not kidding. They're so good you'll have a hard time, even after twenty-five years, getting the voice out of your head. Pay attention to the way the vignettes stir your imagination without too much stage directing: this is a life lesson.

☐ **Speaking of J. Peterman, watch *Comedian*, the Jerry Seinfeld movie.** Pay close attention to the part where the woman asks him if this is his first time doing stand-up.

☐ **When you get back from Mexico, people will probably ask you where you got the tan.** (Imagine you're tan instead of burned. Imagine you're someone else entirely. Imagine that!) Lie to them mercilessly. They don't need to know the truth. No one needs to know the truth. Your job is to create the grandest possible falsity. Think: Marco Polo was a fucking hack.

Now, if none of these work, find a good woman or a dependable man, move to the country, and settle down in a big house. It's not worth it.

CHECK INTO AN

EXPEN$IVE

HOTEL

This only works if you are a little on the cheap side.

Check into an expensive hotel for three nights. It's good if it's near the airport or some other deeply boring location. Bring whatever you need to get hopped up: candy, bourbon, coffee, nicotine patches. Also, pants with an elastic waist. And a stack of books that you love but that you have read at least twice already. Once you've checked in, give the remote to the front desk and instruct them not to give it back to you, no matter how much you beg.

Now. Write ten thousand words. If you feel blocked, just think about all the money you're wasting, sitting there, staring into space like an idiot.

How can you defeat the snarling goblins of creative block? With books, of course. Just grab one. It doesn't matter what sort: science fiction, science fact, pornography (soft, hard, or merely squishy), comic books, textbooks, diaries (of people known or unknown), novels, telephone directories, religious texts—anything and everything will work.

Now, open it to a random page. Stare at a random sentence.

For illustrative purposes, I have in front of me *The Wonderful Story of Henry Sugar* (1977) by Roald Dahl. This copy is a well-read paperback with distinguishedly yellowed pages that I've had since I was old enough to want to run away to live in Willy Wonka's factory. So this book has a smell that's a mixture of attic, spice rack, glove compartment, and dusty lampshade. If you're using a book like that, pause for a moment and inhale the scent. You may have already triggered your brain into pondering new ideas, and, if so, our work here is done. Marvelous! If, though, you're still seeking inspiration, select a sentence from any page.

STARE AT

Now, the page I've opened to is page ninety-seven, and my eyes land on this sentence, just a bit further than halfway down the page: "There was no pain, but the force of it was devastating." Marvelous! And so I close my book, open it again to another page, and find another sentence. This time I land on page forty-six, and my gaze falls on this: "The next morning, I went up to the British Museum in London to see the treasure Gordon Butcher had found."

So now we have two sentences, and that's more than enough to tell a new story, a story Mr. Dahl posthumously and inadvertently wrote for us: "There was no pain, but the force was devastating. The next morning, I went up to the British Museum in London to see the treasure Gordon Butcher had found." I'm prompted now to think of vampires in tweed, satin bow ties, weaponry, cursed jewels, tarnished crowns, congealed blood, anesthetic, espionage, cryptic telegrams, crumbling stone buildings, top hats, jousting, shadows dancing across walls, spider bites, and the Holy Grail. Why not? The short story above could be about anything, anyone, in any time—and none of the thoughts that spring to mind are incorrect answers. Every book holds the seeds of a thousand stories. Every sentence can trigger an avalanche of ideas. Mix ideas across books: one thought from Aesop and one line from Chomsky, or a fragment from the IKEA catalog melded with a scrap of dialog from Kerouac.

A RANDOM

By forcing your mind to connect disparate bits of information, you'll jump-start your thinking, and you'll fill in blank after blank with thought after thought. The goblins of creative block have stopped snarling and have been shooed away, you're dashing down thoughts, and your synapses are

SENTENCE

clanging away in a symphonic burst of ideas. And if you're not, whip open another book. Pluck out another sentence. And ponder mash-ups of out-of-context ideas until your mind wanders and you end up in a new place, a place that no one else has ever visited.

Marvelous.

First, panic. That familiar feeling of anxiety floods in, and a headless-chicken approach takes over. Next, after getting a stern reprimanding from my girlfriend for an attitude that isn't helping the problem, I chill (albeit reluctantly at first). I make some tea, open a beer, get a coffee—a refreshment is in order. If I smoked, I would smoke too.

For me the best way to overcome creative block is with space, going for a walk, distancing myself from the desk. One day I hope I can do this kind of walk somewhere more beautiful than the streets of East London. The side of a lake would be quite nice.

When I'm walking I can think things through, and I talk it through too, with myself and with whoever is nearby. There's really something to be said for the adage "a problem shared is a problem halved," even if you're talking aloud to yourself.

TALK THROUGH IT

Everything inspires me— all the things that happen around me at all times.

I try to take some time off if I feel a lack of inspiration. It's always been best for me to go on vacation for a week or two to just listen and watch, all alone. I listen to music and watch people. Everything inspires me—all the things that happen around me at all times. I need to take a step outside my work and life to find new inspiration.

Learn: Focus on things you don't know as well as the things you do. Learning can be a great way to generate new ideas and to make sure you don't overuse old ones. I started taking composition lessons a few years ago to concentrate on some of the things I glossed over during my music education. On top of making me a better musician, my lessons have exposed me to lots of ideas and techniques that I wouldn't have learned otherwise.

My composition teacher taught me an exercise for building musical muscle. You start with two notes (any notes you want—you can even pick them at random), then you add a note, and another, and another. Each time, you expand the motive into something that sounds good to you. You can turn the line upside down, do it backward, transpose it, etc. At the end of the exercise, you should have created something you like out of nothing. The idea being that you can play with notes like clay—they can be sculpted into whatever you want.

WORK HARD
WORK HARD
WORK HARD

WORK HARD

Work Hard: The author Haruki Murakami wrote about how Raymond Chandler made himself sit at his desk for three hours every day even if he didn't write a word. This kind of discipline allowed him to power through "writer's block" and to build his endurance.

Have Sources of Inspiration and Techniques to Help Out When You Get Stuck: An artist friend of mine told me that whenever she encounters "artist's block," she gets a blank canvas and places her ink-stained hand on it, purposefully spoiling it in order to have something to fix. Before she knows it, she's working.

I keep a folder of sounds and synth presets on my hard drive that I've made, recorded from vinyl or through mics, found, etc. I turn to these sounds if I don't have any immediate ideas and need inspiration. They help get my work flowing and often make their way into my songs.

I'm always on the lookout for new instruments of all kinds. Having new instruments around brings new sounds into my life and encourages me to experiment with them.

I keep playlists of music as inspiration for the various projects I'm working on, which can be a good resource if I'm stuck.

Lastly, Don't Be Afraid of Struggle: My mother keeps a great quote by Bill Withers in her office: "On your way to wonderful you're gonna have to pass through alright."

CAMBIA

DE

CHIP

What has always worked for me is quite simple and can be summarized in three words: *cambia de chip*. "Cambia de chip" is a Spanish expression that translates literally to "change chips," and it offers a fresh start, a new perspective, or a change in your way of thinking or state of mind. If I get stuck, I change chips and do something different or think differently about whatever it is I was doing.

When I was an undergraduate student in London, I often used literal English translations of Spanish idiomatic expressions in conversations, and everyone seemed to understand what I meant. But one day a friend laughed out loud when I spoke the words "change chips." She imagined, literally, a person jumping from one potato chip to another. This image has stuck with me since, and getting stuck has become amusing.

Writing this text on creative block has actually inspired me to take this association further and to produce a small publication about different types and shapes of potato chips reflecting different states of mind. Getting stuck can be surprisingly inspiring.

In the spring of 2003, I found myself experiencing a type of writer's block different than the classic portrait of the writer staring pensively at a blank sheet of paper. In my version, I was able to create, just not anything good. I felt as if I were trying to sew a small button onto a shirt, while wearing boxing gloves.

I wasn't always unhappy with my work, but whenever I was, it was usually because of the same reason: I needed to make the work perfect. I would have a vision in my mind of what I thought the work should be and judge what I made against that imaginary projection.

For me, the creative process is two parts: generating ideas and choosing tools to express those ideas. Both involve skills. The first is of the mind: how to think and organize ideas. The second is of the body: how to use and manipulate materials to express those ideas. Both can be developed and learned, but they are not always aligned with each other.

In art, there is an exercise called blind drawing. It has variations, but the basic premise is that you draw a subject looking only at it, never looking down at the page. This is best done in a short time, such as thirty seconds, and the result is usually a distorted version of the subject. The brilliance of this exercise is that it is impossible to criticize yourself for a blind drawing. With such little time, you are forced to make quick, decisive marks, and the inability to watch those marks as they're happening frees you from criticizing and then altering them. Everyone's blind drawings look like bad drawings, and yet they have a graceful imperfection, giving them an uncanny beauty as well. This was the premise I used to push through the writer's block. →

DRAW A SUBJECT LOOKING ONLY AT IT, NEVER LOOKING DOWN AT THE PAGE

Blind drawing alone was not enough. I needed a working process where I couldn't get in my own way. So I designed a project to bypass my personal critique. I called it Imperfection and the Judgment Machine. Imperfection being that which gives a work its personality, and the Judgment Machine being the critical mind, the force that was hindering me from getting to the beauty of imperfection.

First thing in the studio each morning I drew one self-portrait in the form of a cartoon. This was based on one goal: to draw without thinking—without overthinking. By giving myself the theme, I always had a place to start, and I set a limitation in number to avoid overconceptualizing. I wanted to free myself from expectation, to surprise myself and to take that energy and apply it to the projects I was having trouble with.

Over the course of eight months, I produced more than 130 thematic drawings. I was able to push through and get to a place where I was happy with my work again. The problem-solving exercise made me feel productive and pulled me through the difficulties.

LOOK AT
CREATIVE BLOCK
AS
GROWTH

Over the years I've tried many things to overcome creative block, including not working on a project for a long period of time, going out and having a few hundred beers, cursing and screaming at myself, and even calling to the heavens for answers. Those things never seem to work as well as just beginning the project. As a designer, you're constantly under pressure to do something new, so creative block, unfortunately, is inevitable. I try to stay positive about it and look at creative block as growth—I am not running out of ideas, just trying to push myself into better ones. Anyone who tells you they don't encounter creative block is either not passionate about what they do or is stealing someone else's ideas.

My process for battling creative block is to not prescribe a process for battling creative block. By that I mean no two creative blocks are alike. To assume the same process can cure each and every block would be a little bit nutty, if you ask me.

Sometimes just plowing through a block works great. The more I crank out bad or mediocre ideas, the better are my chances of cranking out good ones eventually. Then again, sometimes that doesn't work.

Sometimes temporarily conceding defeat works well. I leave a design alone for a time, only to return victoriously later in the day or the following day. But sometimes that doesn't work either.

Sometimes just staring at a screen or printed matter works. In fact, I find I tend to stare at my designs, contemplating the rightness or wrongness of them, more than I actually spend time designing those designs. Of course, that doesn't always work.

Sometimes I get lucky and amazing designs slip from my fingers as if fate was in the driver's seat. Rarely does that work for me.

So, how do I overcome creative block? By having several block-curing methods at my disposal rather than a single method. Overcoming blocks is an art, not a science, and we all know art is much more about trial and error than established practices.

WHY NOT TRY

COFFEE

!!

RIGHT BEFORE BED

Creative block is the result of too much thinking. Imagine your brain is like an eight-lane highway: one lane for thoughts about work, another for personal obligations, another for family, and so on. When all the lanes are packed, things are pretty much at a standstill. That mental traffic jam can make it tough to focus on a single creative challenge.

My first tricks for immediately clearing my mind involve things I should do anyway: clean my workspace and make a to-do list. A longer-term strategy is to identify and exploit circumstances that help you clear your mind. Some people get all of their best ideas in the shower. Others swear by coffee shop visits or vintage shopping. Personally, I get lots of ideas on airplanes. Maybe it's the drone of the engine muting my surroundings that helps me concentrate or the fact that I am blissfully unreachable via e-mail for at least a couple of hours. Similarly, I tend to get a lot of good thinking done when I'm on a long drive. The monotony of the road can be very meditative. Plus, it presents a good opportunity to talk to yourself: another focusing trick. Sometimes verbalizing thoughts out loud helps me gain clarity—I'll ask myself questions, respond to them, and then challenge the answers. It may seem a little nutty, but when I finish a long drive, I often have a couple dozen ideas recorded on my phone.

Now, if all this mind-clearing business isn't your cup of tea, why not try coffee—right before bed. It'll do the opposite of everything I've described thus far and likely turn that mental traffic jam into a high-speed demolition derby. Of course, the suggestion of laying in the dark for hours with your pulse and mind racing is terrible medical advice—but hey, I'm not a doctor. Take notes. In the morning, 75 percent will be unintelligible, 20 percent will be laughable, and 5 percent might actually be pretty awesome.

I have never believed that a creative block just happens.

A creative rut is mostly caused by a break in rhythm. After analyzing my own creative frequency, I've found the level of inspiration occurs in waves for me. The lows normally come when my rhythm is disrupted by either a break in process or something else in my life. Just recently, I caught a cold and was feeling rotten. I have no problem sitting at a computer while ill, but it broke my stride because my mood was down, and as a result I couldn't work.

In order to deal with a low point, it's important for me to simplify things. I'll take care of the little things on my to-do list in order to make it appear shorter and more manageable. I'll tidy up my home office so it's more orderly and pleasant to work in, and maybe even tweak my website a bit to tie up loose ends, things I've been meaning to do.

But most importantly, when the management stuff is taken care of, I get away from my computer. If I'm at a low point, the worst thing I can do is sit and stare at the screen or goof around Twitter. So I'll go for a walk to clear my head and ponder the fun projects that I want to do. I'll leave my phone at home so I'm not compelled to check my e-mail while waiting to cross the road.

Another great way to get away from the computer is to grab my sketchbook and head to a coffee shop or local watering hole to do some drawing. Drawing has always been my favorite pastime, because a lot of times it's without focus. I draw for the pleasure of drawing, and I draw whatever I want: Superman, a tree, the A-Team van—it doesn't matter. After about an hour of drawing, it's really easy for me to slip into the groove of coming up with ideas, so I'll shift to sketching poster ideas or something for a client-based project. It's very much about mood. When I'm having a good time, things happen more naturally. Sometimes I'll bring my favorite poster book with me to look at awesome stuff.

I have never believed that a creative block just happens. There's normally a reason why—like I'm stressed about money, just got dumped, or whatever. Once I discover what the reason is, dealing with it is pretty straightforward—for me, anyway.

I do something else.

One of the few benefits of being a freelance writer is that there is always something else I need to do. A blog post, a tweet, a book review. A chapter needs editing or a paper needs grading. Or, since I work from home, there's dishwashing, laundry folding, lunch making. When I was writing my dissertation, I did a lot of baking and candying. But once I am at my desk, I prefer to stay there, so I am more likely to move from one thing to another only in my mind. I leave myself a Post-it each night of what I should do the next day, and as if I were my own boss, I let myself move freely among the items on that list. There's always something that seems more appealing than the window I have open on screen, and that's the thing I choose.

Then, while I am doing that second thing, a better idea for the first thing usually comes to mind. I will jot that idea down on my yellow pad, so it doesn't get scared away by the computer, and go on with the second thing. Because almost all of my work is

DO SOMETHING

ELSE

on the computer, my Post-its and my yellow pad act as a staging
area. Ideas there can be more vague, and later I will go back
and annotate them on the page before transferring them to their
official window. Because of the superstitious nature of this process,
I am very picky about my pads and my pens and the dimensions
and color of my Post-its.

A corollary of this habit is that if I don't have enough things to do,
I get very nervous. That nervousness turns into a rattling-around
sort of energy—energy that causes me to throw out old toys, to make up
bags to take to the Goodwill, and to send too many e-mails. But some
of those e-mails contain ideas for the next list of things to do.

Being nervous makes me bolder about asking people for help
and proposing new projects. When everything is humming along, I feel
like my work is more ordinary and I don't challenge myself. If there
are three things on the list, why rock the boat? It is when the Post-it
is blank that I really get creative.

- PAINT THE BARN
- MOW THE HAYFIELD
- PICK BLUEBERRIES
- CUT FIREWOOD
- RAKE LEAVES
- SHOVEL SNOW
- CLEAN THE BASEMENT

My strategy for getting myself out of a rut is to sit at my desk reminding myself of what the problem is, reviewing my notes, generally filling my head with the issues and terms, and then I just get up and go do something relatively mindless and repetitive. At our farm in the summer, I paint the barn or mow the hayfield or pick blueberries or cut firewood to length; and at home in Massachusetts in the winter, I rake leaves or shovel snow or clean the basement floor. I don't even try to think about the problem, but more often than not, at some point in the middle of the not very challenging activity, I'll find myself mulling it over and coming up with a new slant, a new way of tackling the issue, maybe just a new term to use. Engaging my brain with something else to control and think about helps melt down the blockades that have been preventing me from making progress, freeing up the circuits for some new paths. My strategy could hardly be cruder, but it works so well so often that I have come to rely on it.

One summer many years ago, my friend Doug Hofstadter was visiting me at my farm, and somebody asked him where I was. He gestured out to the big hayfield behind the house, which I was harrowing for a reseeding. "He's out there on his tractor, doing his tillosophy," Doug said. Ever since then, tillosophy has been my term for this process. Try it; if it doesn't work, at least you'll end up with a painted room, a mowed lawn, a clean basement.

Remember
that creative block
is normal.

I can't say I have a secret for overcoming creative block besides
patience—or I should say trying to be patient and trying to remember
that creative block is normal. I can't say I enjoy the process of
being stuck, but over time I've learned to accept it and do my best
to work through it.

CREATIVE PROCESS
ANALYSIS FORM **13**

SUBJECT: Joe Haller & Ian Hannula	STUDY: Creative process
COMPANY: Nice Collective	PROCESSING DATE: 09/28/11
	PERIOD OF ANALYSIS: 01/01/1998 - 09/01/2011

5) COGNITIVE PROCESS *(check top three choices)*
- ☐ Explicit
- ☑ Implicit
- ☐ Analytical/ critical
- ☐ Evolution
- ☑ Synthesis
- ☐ Adaptive /resourceful
- ☑ Innovative/ Original
- ☐ Reapplication

6) INSPIRATION / MOTIVATION *(check all that apply)*
- ☑ Self competition
- ☑ Curiosity
- ☐ Challenge
- ☐ Reward/praise
- ☐ Fear/disapproval
- ☑ Intrinsic
- ☑ Extrinsic
- ☑ Time constraints
- ☐ Freedom
- ☐ Comparative competition
- ☑ Constructive discontent
- ☐ Anger

7) STIMULUS *(check top two choices)*
- ☐ Imagination
- ☐ Social interaction
- ☐ Solitude
- ☐ Art
- ☐ Nature
- ☑ Science
- ☐ Visual stimuli
- ☐ Environment
- ☑ Auditory stimuli (music /sound effects)

8) IDEA SOURCE *(check top two choices)*
- ☐ Novelty
- ☑ Indirect source
- ☐ Direct source
- ☐ Familiarity
- ☑ Curiosity
- ☐ External information specifically gathered
- ☑ Internal memories and perspective from natural absorption
- ☑ Inclination for problem solving

9) TOOLS FOR REGAINING MOMENTUM *(check all that apply)*
- ☑ Direction shift
- ☐ Reference Material
- ☐ Pause / Break
- ☐ Alternate project
- ☐ Meditation
- ☐ Physical Activity
- ☐ Increase Focus
- ☑ Increase effort / investment
- ☐ Diversion / Distration from 3rd party
- ☐ Cleaning Busy work

FINDINGS:

The study was unable to prove the existence of creative block as a disorder or a condition unto itself. Periods of reduced output are a natural component in the fluctuating cycles of the creative process.

Creativity requires conditioning, intellectual skills, discipline and preparation. It was found to be similar in many ways to how an athlete achieves peak performance through training, lifestyle and daily diligence. For both creatives and athletes alike, optimum output is achieved only when focus is evoked and applied to previous physical or intellectual investment. Having creativity at one's disposal, and the ability to access it freely, is generated by nurturing the complex relationship between oneself and the world around them. Openness, self confidence, a willingness to explore, autonomy, balance, and intuition are key components which allow creativity to flourish. Acute perception, skillful filtering and a commitment to simplicity were found to yield the most successful results.

Further findings revealed that the more someone diversified their experience and expanded their scope of knowledge, the more reliable their intuition became. Innovation appears to be a discipline.

VISU ALLY BOM BARD MYSELF

When dealing with a creative block, I try to find a way into the core of my mind where all my ideas swirl around. I always start out by listening to music. Ambient, electronic, and motion-picture soundtracks/scores get me in a certain mood and state of mind where all my creative juices start flowing. The list is endless, but Sigur Rós and Hammock have by far been some of my biggest sources of inspiration.

I try to delve in and find the mood that will play a key role in my work. In the process of dealing with my creative block, I tend to look back, to the time when I was young and read every issue of *Cinefex*, dreaming of special effects in my sleep and of one day becoming a star in my artistic field. Back to the sense of feeling special and that you are blessed with a unique gift—the gift to create. That unaffected attitude and open-minded creativeness that I enjoyed as a youngster I try to mimic in my creative process. It's like entering a pod that travels back and forth in time through my creative mind until it finds its destination.

I also visually bombard myself by looking through endless magazines, blogs, movies, and such for inspiration. It helps me nail down the exact mood and story I want to tell in my work. I usually look through work from directors such as David Fincher, David Lynch, Ridley Scott, Stanley Kubrick, and Steven Spielberg—just to name a few—for reference. I read architectural magazines en masse in order to feed my brain with aesthetics, compositions, lines, angles, forms, and patterns.

Travel always stirs the inner reaches of creativity. Even a half-hour walk outside of the workspace provides sights and sounds and stimulus different than the drudge of routine or familiar places.

Another trick to switch up a dull creative mood is to clean up the work environment. A full day doing nothing but organizing and cleaning the studio always provides a fresh perspective. Even just sweeping the floor helps sometimes.

Also, conversation. Really good conversation stimulates my brain and can get me all fired up about a project. I think this is why creative folks habituate bars and cafes—it's for the conversation. There's nothing like a long debate with a peer to get the old synapses going.

I love researching. I don't play board games or video games because history and researching thoroughly occupy my mind and imagination. Researching always sparks a new idea, and if it is not germane to a current project, I file it away for later. I'd say 20 percent of my stored ideas become real projects at some point in my life.

The last and most used trick for me these days to overcome creative block is to write, write anything that comes to mind. Just getting thoughts out on the page helps. I find the process of writing a perfect combination of pure creativity and structure; for me, it seems to combine the functions of right and left brain, which is incredibly satisfying and productive.

JUST SWEEPING THE FLOOR HELPS SOMETIMES

Creative Bollocks

"Wait without thought, for you
are not ready for thought."
—T. S. Eliot, "East Coker"

When I was a little boy, I would
close my eyes and often see
before me the skin of a bright
yellow tiger. I never tried to share
this experience. It was what it
was: at once frightening and
deeply solitary. My guess now is
that the bright yellow and black
coloring of the tiger's skin was
only certain light passing through
my eyelids. No matter. The tiger
is long gone.

Beethoven drank buckets
of strong, black coffee. Beethoven
was creatively prodigious.
(He also went deaf and, perhaps,
mad.) Sound syllogism here?
I'd like to think so.

The idea that creativity
is some abundantly available
resource waiting simply for the
right application of ingenuity
to extract, refine, and pipe it into

WHAT'S WRONG WITH CREATIVE BLOCK?

the grid seems so axiomatic at this cultural juncture that the very distinction between creativity and productivity has been effectively erased.

And so it is that, when faced with a decreased flow in productivity, we ask not what it might be that's interfering with our creative process, but rather what device might be quickly employed to raise production levels. This is standard, myopic symptomatology-over-pathology response, typical of a pressurized environment of dislocated self-entitlement. (See "quick fix.")

At the risk of going off brief here, can I just ask: What's wrong with creative block? Might it not just be that periods—even extended ones—of productive hiatus are essential mechanisms of gestation designed to help us attain higher standards in our pursuit of creative excellence? Because let's be honest. While we're hardly short on creativity, we're not exactly banging out masterpieces.

White bird: A child does not get creative block.

Blue bird: A child is not productive.

White bird: A child is productive, just not logical.

Blue bird: A child does not need to make ends meet.

(Anecdote): John Harrison took decades in obscure isolation to conceive and build his H4 clock. This precision marine chronometer, which finally gave navigators the tool to know their longitude and thus their position on the globe, saved countless souls from a watery end and revolutionized maritime industry and the charting of our planet.

On second thought, big pharma makes billions every year treating symptomatology. (After all, you can't drink four ⟶

hundred million cups of coffee a day and expect not to have an upset stomach—which is, incidentally, why Procter & Gamble, purveyors of Pepto-Bismol, also own Folgers.)

Beethoven had an upset stomach.

So, in the spirit of fulfilling demand and prescription, here's a top-ten list:

- ☐ Take all clocks and watches from the house.
- ☐ Mirrors too, while you're at it.
- ☐ If you live near a body of very cold water, jump in it.
- ☐ Do not think of the future.
- ☐ Perceive your audience as the enemy.
- ☐ Don't eat for a while.
- ☐ Pick up photographs of strangers at your local junk shop.
- ☐ Remember there are exactly 168 hours in the week.
- ☐ Download "Creativity app" to your phone.
- ☐ If nothing else works, try severing your index finger at the first knuckle.

*I drank five cups of espresso to write this.

The key is to sketch quickly, without getting caught up in the execution or technique.

Lots of reading and lots of sketching. The reading part is a long-term strategy: constantly consuming ideas, influences, details, angles, metaphors, symbols, etc., and storing them in the back of your brain so that later on—sometimes much later on—you have a rich catalog of starting points to draw from. Sketching is a way to activate all of that background information when faced with a problem: the act of drawing, of giving visual expression to many different ideas, helps you sort through all of those random elements and to make unexpected connections between them. The key is to sketch quickly, without getting caught up in the execution or technique. That way you stay in the realm of content, without getting bogged down.

Most designers will tell you that they have a number of strategies for overcoming creative block, and for the most part many of the approaches are similar. The most popular of them seem to be listening to music, reading, walking, and sketching. What these have in common is that they don't force you to tackle the problem but rather encourage trying to relax the mind by stepping away from the issues at hand.

Inspiration is everywhere, often found in the oddest of places, and it's important that you take nothing for granted and absorb as much as you can from your surroundings. When you have the time to chill and let your mind wander more of these stored inspirations will be released, helping you overcome any creative blocks.

Personal creative block tips: I'm a creature of habit, like most people, but it's important to occasionally mix things up and do something different once in a while (for example, walk a different way home or read a magazine you wouldn't usually read).

Anyone who follows me on Flickr will know I am at the beach more times than the lifeguard. For me this is where I am most relaxed and where my mind can wander freely. It's very important to find your beach—wherever that may be—and go there as often as possible.

Always have a notebook on you, even if you don't have any thoughts to jot down—just doodling can often bring about new ideas. I rarely do sketch work for projects that I'm working on, but anyone who has seen my notebooks knows they are full of doodles, and they are invaluable when I'm in a jam.

Get a cat. I've lost count the number of times my late cat Dillon helped me with my creative block by distracting me and by relaxing as only cats can.

Take notes every time you face creative block and look for patterns. I've noticed a trend of getting them on Mondays.

Continuously thinking about a problem that needs to be solved can be very draining. There is a point I reach when I know I cannot possibly come up with a solution if I keep on thinking about it. Ultimately, overcoming this usually involves some form of distraction, away from my computer screen.

Working from home means that I can go and sort things out around the house that need tending to. I also like to make something very elaborate and repetitive in the kitchen—preparing vegetables and making some sort of comfort food, such as lasagna. There is something I find very rewarding about making lasagna, and it makes me feel like I have achieved something, even though I have not necessarily solved my creative block.

If that distraction doesn't help, then I go for a walk in the park. Seeing other people go about their lives helps relax me and clear my mind. Sometimes just getting a bit of sun on my skin can really help too.

Finally, if all else fails, one of the most powerful forms of distraction is going to the cinema. There is something about being in a darkened room that forces me to stop worrying and totally become involved with the story that is unfolding on screen. I usually feel very refreshed, like someone has reset my brain, which inspires me to start thinking about my project again.

MAKE SOMETHING

VERY
ELABORATE

☆☆☆☆☆☆☆☆☆☆☆☆☆☆☆☆☆☆☆☆☆
☆☆☆☆☆☆☆☆☆☆☆☆☆☆☆☆☆☆☆☆☆
☆☆☆☆☆☆☆☆☆☆☆☆☆☆☆☆☆☆☆☆☆

|||||||||||||||||||| & ||||||||||||||||||||

REPETITIVE

IN THE KITCHEN

FREE

LET THE MIND FLOAT

It's not about having techniques for overcoming a creative block, it's all about stimulating mental states that allow me to think creatively. I don't feel like I "make" the ideas, I "get" them—they're already there, I just have to allow them to surface.

In order to approach something truly creatively, I need to let go of specifics and, with a general notion peripherally in mind, let the mind float free. There's so much activity happening right below the waking surface, and ideas simply start bubbling up. There are a variety of mental states that work particularly well for this, like (day)dreaming, meditation, hallucination, trance, hypnosis, psychedelic states, physical exertion, etc.

So my best strategy when facing a creative challenge is to not think about it directly at all, but to let the mind do what it does naturally. I usually take my time to let things run their course: it can take hours, or days, sometimes weeks, depending on the scale of the situation. It happens when it happens. Some people call this procrastination; but to me it's a necessary and important part of the creative process. (And it helps to have flexible deadlines. I don't work on too many projects that start with a problem. I usually work on things because I "got" an idea, which is a great antidote against creative block.)

It's not always practical to just drop everything and start working on something else. Sometimes the project just has to get done.

As a designer and musician, I've always had the two outlets to spark my creativity.

I think it's important to find another creative outlet to keep you motivated and practicing when the first is stagnant. When I hit the wall in design, I start creating a lot of music and vice versa. When I pour myself into a project for any extended period of time, I have a tendency to focus too much on details and not the overall spirit of the work; focusing my creative energy on something else for a while helps me see things for what they are when I return.

Of course, it's not always practical to just drop everything and start working on something else. Sometimes the project just has to get done. In these cases, exercise is a very effective way to quickly clear my head and find the perspective I need. I've always been amazed at how differently I approach a problem when I've had a chance to get out of the studio and engage in physical activity. I prefer running and cycling to help work through sticking points— something about that type of monotony and exertion clears up a part of my mind and helps me work through the real issues of a project.

- Start working on anything. It can turn out lame and ugly. But you'll have achieved something, and now it's usually much easier to go on.

- Accept that you're off mode. Wait it out and use the time to feed your mind with things you might be able to use later. Don't be too picky. Any experience can be an asset.

- Pull out something old and tune it or recycle it. This can be some old picture you used to work on or your bike.

STOP CREATING

- Change your working method. Use your left hand, for example. Try some new software.

- Configure the document you're working on into the start-up items on your computer. Every morning when you start your machine, it will pop up in front of you.

- Publish your sketches. Getting exposure might motivate you. Don't go for quality, think about turning yourself on.

- Stop creating. Why not? Be a happy consumer and support creators! You can change roles anytime!

- As a last resort, get as bored as possible. Don't try to distract yourself. There's a good chance you'll absolutely want and need to start working after some time.

- Enjoy your depression.

BLOC

Asked about the notion of the "creative block," we can't help but notice the interesting relationship between the words *block* and *bloc*.

Block, when used in a phrase such as "writer's block," obviously refers to the idea of a psychological blockade—an obstruction or obstacle that somehow arose between the writer (or artist or designer) and his/her ability to create. As for the word *bloc*, we here specifically refer to the way it is used in the phrase "black bloc." A black bloc is a certain tactic used by ad hoc groups of anarchists and autonomists during protests and marches. (Be sure to google "book bloc" for a particularly fascinating variation on this tactic.) An important role of the black bloc is to break through barriers created by the riot police.

So while the word *block* refers to an actual barricade, the word *bloc* points to a tactic to overcome this barricade. And while *block* signifies passivity, *bloc* describes a more active (and activist) attitude.

In other words, next time you have to deal with creative block, just drop that *k*, and turn it into a creative bloc. Most philosophical problems can be solved within the linguistic sphere—this is one of them.

Creative block causes a sickening feeling. It's something that is inevitable, depressing, and exciting all at once. A challenge lies ahead, but one that seems remarkably more difficult than it ever did before. Herein lies the real issue, though: you are a professional artist. You must create fresh ideas, on demand, and with very little margin of poor taste. And unless you're independently wealthy, you've got deadlines to meet and bills to pay. This is when creative block goes from problem to emergency.

Every artist has a bag of tricks to beat creative block, methods that have been developed over the years. In my case, I've developed a three-tiered pyramid, and each level's size and position represents the amount of time and resources it takes to return to normalcy, as well as the emergency level that I currently face.

The top level of the pyramid, the point, is the smallest of the three. It holds the go-to material. All unused ideas and inspirational clippings reside here. With the number of rejected ideas that have accumulated over the years, there is usually enough to at least jump-start something new.

The next level is the panic level. It sits right smack in the middle and usually consists of the most amount of whining. Take a step away from work, run some errands, watch some TV, and grab something to eat. Come back with a fresh mind, and give it another go. With the stress that comes along with being a professional, it's natural to have an overloaded and overworked brain, and sometimes, when you can't just power through a block, you need to take some time to reboot.

The final level is all about regrouping. The time for panic is over, and now it's about making things happen. Symbolically speaking, the bottom is not only a last-ditch effort, but also the largest piece

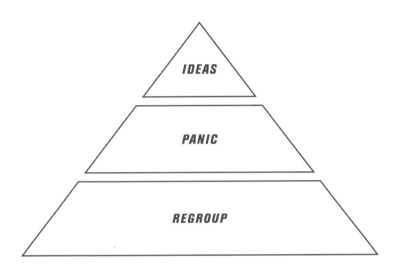

of the pyramid, so it houses the most options to get you back on track. This is the stage at which you must pry yourself away from all of the usual day-to-day tasks and technologies and get back to basics. Visit a museum, go to an antiques shop or a used bookstore—anywhere that you can see the birth of a truly creative idea. It may take up the most amount of time, but it'll be worth it.

Living and breathing true creativity should not only get you past your block, it will give you a whole new arsenal of ideas to float you far into the future. By the next time creative block rears its ugly head, you will be thoroughly prepared and the feeling of overwhelming anxiety will be substantially smaller. What a relief.

On one occasion, I set out to make a perfect sculptural replica of my hands and feet with plaster molds. Creatively, I was determined to do it, but the idea of the final product seemed kind of lame. Not only did I have no idea how to get it done, I had no interest in learning how to do it. This was an awkward position to be in but also a familiar one. It happens all too often, a conflict between the joy of the process and the uncertainty of the outcome.

But not this time. I gathered the plaster and tools I needed. I built some cube molds out of plywood, a bit bigger than my hands and feet. I mixed up the plaster with a small part concrete (for a faster set). I poured it into the molds, stuck my hands and feet in, and waited. I spent the next three days and two nights with white plaster cubes solidifying around the ends of my limbs. The cubes were heavy. I needed a lot of help from people around me just to get through the day. My hands and feet had no way of expanding in the cubes as blood would rush in and out, causing a strange and painful pressure. In the forty-seventh hour, I had to have a friend chip them off with a pair of metal scissors and a mini baseball bat. The three days were documented on video. Dubbed the *Plaster Blocks Project*, this is one of my favorite artworks I have created.

Solidifying your hands and feet in plaster blocks is not, however, a silver bullet remedy for creative block. Here is my suggestion: when we run into problems with our work, we should really run into them. We should run as fast as we can, like sprinting head first into a concrete wall.

WHEN
WE RUN
INTO
PROBLEMS
WITH OUR
WORK
WE
SHOULD
REALLY
RUN INTO
THEM.

It has always been part of the creative process to have moments when you think that you're not going to make it. During these times when you feel sick to your stomach—for hours, even days—you walk around, cleaning your desk, doing the laundry, or making unusual sculptures with objects on your desk. It feels like procrastinating, and it is sometimes painful, but it really needs to happen to fully enjoy the final piece.

While each project is different, there are still some guidelines I tend to follow:

- ☐ **Talk with someone about it.** It doesn't matter if it's a colleague or a friend—just explain the problem, and they might come up with a solution that sparks a brilliant idea.

- ☐ **Take pictures, write, and sketch.** I always keep notes of ideas I have while grocery shopping or watching a movie. It's a precious collection of impressions that might fit or guide you toward what you are seeking. While looking for the perfect concept, some insignificant thoughts might come. Note them— they will be useful later for another project.

- ☐ **Try to create blindly.** One way to disconnect with the exact purpose of what you need to do is to take an insignificant object and use it as an actor in this project. Allow yourself latitude. You can waste a lot of time doing so, but what really matters here is keeping the imagination going.

- ☐ **Do the obvious.** There is often a first image that comes to mind when you think about a new project. It sticks in your mind, and you can't stop thinking about it. Even when you know it's shit, just do it. And then throw it out.

I believe creative block is closely connected to fear: fear of my ideas not being good enough. When I find myself in a rut, it's usually because I've started losing confidence in my idea. I start destroying the path behind me, and my brain wants to come up with a new one, because it seeks something easier. When I recognized this pattern, I found that I could use these moments as tools. When the process starts slowing down and my concentration drops—when fear has kicked in—they very often signal that I'm onto something of value, and I have to push through.

Creative block is probably best described as being in a constant state of fear, corrupting my mind while attempting to destroy my ideas. Fight it!

Wikipedia offers a deep well of mediated randomness.

As the execution of my artwork takes a very long time, I typically have more ideas than I know what to do with. When I'm stuck, however, and looking for a little inspiration, I have a two-pronged approach: old sketchbooks and Wikipedia.

My sketchbooks, numbered and lined up on a shelf in my office, are filled with scraps of ideas—sometimes a sketch, sometimes just a stray sentence—I've gathered over the course of the last decade or so. From a distance of years, many of these ideas seem simple, naive, or antiquated, but some of them still resonate enough to jump-start new works. Furthermore, as evidence that inspiration and excitement existed in the past, these older ideas offer reassurance to the present and future.

For generating ideas, I find that Wikipedia offers a deep well of mediated randomness, taking me down long paths I never knew existed. As I write this, I pause to click on "Random article," which brings me to an article on "Thomas H. McNeil," which contains a hyperlink to "secret society," which in turn takes me to "secret knowledge," "secrecy," or "conspiracy theory"—any of which might yield a spark for something new. At the core of this exercise is curiosity—seeking out the information and ideas that interest me most, while giving myself over to chance.

BOOKS!

Whenever I have creative block, I always go to look at books. These are usually photography books and usually from my library, which I started in 1988 (at eighteen years old) when I bought my first photo book in Pittsburgh, Pennsylvania.

I have my photo books very carefully organized by genre in my home studio—in groups like conceptual art, painting, portraiture, landscape, architecture, still life, night photography, documentary and street photography, film, books on books, design. I even have a section on all kinds of police and medical pictures. By cruising through these books that I have lovingly brought into my world, I usually find many sparks of inspiration that get me back on track.

This collection is something that I've shared with countless students over the last fifteen years that I've been teaching in the Bay Area. I usually show up with two big canvas bags of photo books that I let the students go through each week. In the process of carrying them back and forth, some of my favorites have become dog-eared, but I don't really care about that. I'm only interested in the messages that can be conveyed to my students through them. I know that they prefer looking at real books over an often-pixelated PowerPoint presentation on the topic of the week.

So the answer is BOOKS!

I try to learn from my pursuits outside of the studio. For example, if I am stuck in front of a computer screen, I might get up and build something with my hands. I like to solder components and construct my own audio equipment. The process is visceral and industrious. In creating my own tools, I begin to see them as pieces of art. In viewing these tools as art, I begin to see a side of my creative process that is methodical and mechanical and one that can help me overcome a creative hurdle.

I also like to cook and I find the experimentation and addition of individual ingredients analogous to my compositional style. Forays in woodworking, graphic design, programming, or interactive installation also inform my primary craft. These pursuits allow me to clear my mind while granting a fresh insight into how I create music and audio.

Through a diverse range of projects, I experiment with a range of media and creative techniques. When I hit the metaphorical wall, I can quickly jump to another project that uses a different set of tools and rewards a different set of ideas. It seems that the more work I generate, the more frequently I fail. The more frequently I fail, the more effective I become at avoiding block. And the more effective I become, the more likely I am to succeed when the next project comes around.

BUILD SOMETHING WITH YOUR HANDS

LET GRAVIT PULL YOU Y

D

O

W

N

I used to race mountain bikes when I was a lot younger, and one of the most valuable lessons I learned while tackling some of the larger, more technical hills was to not overthink the challenge—to just let gravity pull me down and allow my body to negotiate the roots of trees, the steep inclines, holes. The moments when I hesitated were always the times when I ended up over the handlebars.

I follow the very same philosophy in writing music: I simply commit to the act of writing, not resisting any particular direction the song takes me. I let the gravity of that composition pull me into it. I trust my creative abilities to carry me to the end of the process—unscathed.

The tactical system that I have created for myself is so that I won't miss out on any particular inspirational moments—so nothing will be standing in the way of actually recording an idea. You never know when a really strong idea will hit. I always have my recording equipment set up close to where I sleep, not a single cable unplugged. If I am not at home, I'll sing ideas into my iPad or phone—I never just ruminate on an idea if it can be avoided.

Since I write very journalistic types of songs, I have a strict policy of not being scared to live life. I allow myself to fall in love, to be upset, to be happy, to indulge in the sensual pleasures that life has to offer. There are years of inspiration tucked away in the day-to-day experiences that make up my life. These moments fuel my songs, and I often try to find ways to include these in the songs I create.

Don't judge your own work if it's not coming out the way you want. Don't stop yourself before you have even started. Keep on until it feels right again. As long as you are enjoying the actual process, you are in a good place. Creative expression is like a love affair—you do it because it drives you, it excites you.

As a product designer, most of what I do is twofold: understand the problem I want to solve and approach it from as many angles as I can. After executing on a well-defined and accurately constrained problem in multiple ways, it soon becomes obvious what the true or best solution is. Creative block generally arises from a breakdown in this process.

If you're stuck in the middle of the design, it probably means that you're not asking enough questions. Who is the audience? What do they feel? What do they desire? What will improve their life and create joy? How do other designers tackle similar problems? At the core of every successful design is a set of simply defined constraints that you measure your ideas against. It's all about determining the soul of a product before laying down the first pixel or pen stroke.

Using constraints and understanding as a foundation, you should then execute as many variations you can within those bounds. There are limitless ways to tackle a problem both functionally and aesthetically, which is why you need to uncover a wide spectrum of possibilities to see what feels right. This is crucial to determining quality. Creating various options also means that you don't need to put pressure on yourself to form one perfect solution from the start. Explore the good and explore the bad—creative block does not exist here, because even a bad direction can move you closer to the right one.

Accurately understand your task and explore immediately. Give yourself the space to freely fail, and that same space will give you the freedom to succeed.

EXPLORE THE GOOD & *EXPLORE THE BAD*

THE MUNDANENESS OF NAVIGATION THINGS CENTER OF HELPS ME SEE THE

I don't think in terms of *creative* and *block*, but—to show that I'm not trying to be a pain—let me explain, and then I'll say something useful.

First of all, being creative is not summoning stuff *ex nihilo*. It's work, plain and simple—adding something to some other thing or transforming something. In the work that I do, as a writer and a metaphor designer, there's always a way to get something to do something to do something else. No one talks about work block.

Also, *block* implies a hydraulic metaphor of thinking. Thoughts flow. Difficulty thinking represents impeded flow. This interpretation also suggests a single channel for that flow. A stopped pipe. A dammed river. If you only have one channel, one conduit, then you're vulnerable to blockage. Trying to solve creative block, I imagine a kind of psychic Roto-Rootering.

My conceptual scheme is more about the temperature of things: I try to find out what's hot and start there, even if it may be unrelated to what I need to be working on, and most of the time, that heats up other areas too. You can solve a lot with a new conceptual frame.

So here are some things I do to heat things up. I talk about what I'm doing. Putting a real person, instead of a blinking cursor and a screen, on the other end of the interaction gives me access to different articulations. Movement helps. Something about the mundaneness of navigation helps me see to the center of things. Going for a walk, traveling on a plane. Also, trying to imagine how someone else would solve the problem, then trying to execute that in his or her voice. I ask myself, what would Dave Hickey do?

SIT DOWN SHUT UP GO OFF-LINE

Getting stuck is a big part of creative work, and it's really important to be good at getting unstuck. There are two main reasons why creative people get stuck on a piece of work. The first is you don't actually have an idea. You may have requirements, and you may have tools. But you don't actually have an idea that's going to carry the day, and you're going to be stuck until you get a solid idea. The second reason creative people get stuck is that, while they have the idea, executing the idea takes a lot of work, and not all of that work is fun, and basically you don't want to do the work, because having the idea in the first place was the fun part. The problem is you don't get to say "check mate in four." You actually have to finish the project. So you get mystically "stuck" after the brilliant sketch is done.

It is very, very important to accurately understand which of these problems you're having when you get stuck. If you don't have an idea, you need to play around a little, take a walk, have a good conversation, open the aperture. As they say in drawing class, explore the negative space. If you're balking at the work, you need to stop playing around, sit down, shut up, go off-line, focus single-mindedly on executing the work, and make it real. In either case, if you try to solve one problem when you're really having the other, you're going to waste a lot of time.

Commencement speech given at the Ringling College of Art and Design, 2011.

I try to avoid working late.

Usually when I'm in a creative rut, I find myself spacing out. So I'll get up and move around a little. If that doesn't work, I will change my environment. I'll go outside or to a coffee shop. The best ideas I have usually are not conceived in an office.

I'll also change up what I'm looking at. My favorite book that helps kick-start my brain is *The Art of Looking Sideways* (2001) by Alan Fletcher. It's an amazing book with all sorts of thoughts and visuals. I also keep a folder full of inspirational or funny quotes, pictures, typography, illustrations, etc., to help get me out of a rut.

I try to avoid working late. I'll be grumpy, and it won't do anything for me except make my next day unproductive. I also try to not put too much pressure on myself. It takes up time and energy and won't get me anywhere.

Sometimes it's just about getting something down on paper, good or bad. Something is better than nothing. It's okay to fail. I always try to remember the age-old idea articulated by Woody Allen: "If you're not failing every now and again, it's a sign you're not doing anything very innovative."

FREE YOUR MIND

Creative block makes me feel like I'm stuck in an empty white cube without shadows or surfaces—just a blank void. Generally, the cause of this is because I'm trying to force an idea into something that doesn't fit it—I'm thinking myself into the box. Over time, I have discovered that it is simply a matter of letting go, and the box will break itself down.

In both professional and personal work, getting into a flow is the key to my creativity: it allows my past experiences and emotions to click in from a place beyond rational thought and steers me toward something greater than the initial idea. This is an oversimplification, but it is similar to when you blank on a person's name. You can sit and think so hard that your blood vessels will burst, but the moment you free your mind and think of something else, the name pops right up.

Also, taking a break to play with my dog helps.

To *be* is to *do* —Socrates
To *do* is to *be* —Sartre
Do be do be do —Sinatra
—From *Subway* (1985)

To *be* is to *do* —Socrates

Typically, the first thing I do when I hit a creative block is to take a break. Only it's never actually a real break. Once I've been confronted with a design problem, I can never push the problem entirely out of my head. It's always there, nibbling away at me, a kind of incredibly consuming obsession. Maybe that's a good thing. I'm not sure. However, what that means is that I'm always in some way switched on and conscious of the connections between my thoughts and the particular design problem.

It's with this in mind that I simply try to enjoy the process of whatever I happen to be doing at the time. It lets me reset and refresh my headspace, allowing new perspectives on the world to come and go freely.

I tend to walk everywhere. It forces me to slow down, take in the people and things that I wouldn't ordinarily register. In particular, I absolutely love people watching. A conversational extract existing briefly in the street before trailing off down the road is an engaging occurrence for me. The unfinished sentiment always leaves a lot to the imagination.

To *do* is to *be* —Sartre

Pushing through the block can also be an important part of the process. Making that start, without expecting to fire that one →

IT'S NECESSARY TO

MAKE A MESS

silver bullet. It can be the hardest part, but it's important to just get in there and experiment, even when things are not feeling particularly inspired. It's necessary to make a mess, often trying even seemingly irrelevant or tangential things. Sometimes beautiful things can happen when you just throw yourself out there. When I do this, there's usually one thing, often a minute detail, that will kick-start me and remind me why I love doing what I do.

*Do be do be do —*Sinatra
Alternatively, eating a ridiculous amount of cheese before bedtime and relying on your dreams doesn't hurt. I've managed to solve many a problem through restless dream-filled nights. Working in my sleep is an efficient use of my time. Being and doing.

ONCE AN IDEA IS ON PAPER

ANOTHER IS FREE TO PRESENT ITSELF

My strategy is pretty unconscious. If I go looking for inspiration and try too hard, it doesn't always happen. But having said that, I have found that the most stimulating condition is going to a foreign city—not necessarily abroad, although I think that helps.

Spend a day mooching—shops are sometimes better than art galleries! You must be on your own all day. Have a notebook and a pen. When you have spent a day visiting all sorts of places, go and have a meal or a beer or a coffee—whatever you want, but you need to be relaxed and unrushed. I find that these are the times when ideas flow. Stimulated by all you have seen, write down everything that comes into your head—don't reject ideas and refuse to write them down, you don't have to use them! Writing down everything creates a flow: once an idea is on paper, another is free to present itself to you. Last time I did this, I had more ideas than I could use in a year!

What's the problem?

Robert Frost wrote of the "road less traveled," and as creative professionals that's the one we often seek. The natural tendency of designers is to eschew the familiar in pursuit of the adventure, but sometimes the well-trodden path is worn for a reason. Sometimes it's the better choice. When you find yourself at these moments of indecision, ask yourself: "Am I really stuck?" Sometimes we think

we're stuck (or want to think we're stuck), but we're actually on track and just don't know it. Some paths are inevitable. Remember, a rut is also a groove.

Being stuck can feel like being at a creative crossroads: you see the paths in front of you but don't know which one to choose. This has to do with fear of making the wrong decision.

When fear isn't the problem, clarity often is. The inability to make a decision usually has less to do with not knowing the answer and more to do with not knowing the question. This kind of being stuck is about not seeing the problem clearly. The best medicine for that is perspective. Perspective can be measured in units of time and distance. Getting away from a problem helps provide a better view of it. Instead of flailing away at something you can't really see, try doing something unrelated. Inevitably, something from the other experience will present itself as the answer to the problem you're trying to ignore. Remember to build in some away time.

While fear and lack of clarity can be powerful limiters, lack of confidence is both more common and more crippling. The only remedy for this is to become awesome. We all face problems to which the solutions are clear but executing the answers seems too difficult. To get over that hurdle, work on other, easier tasks first. They don't have to be related—doing some touch-up painting around the office, finishing a blog post, or color-coding your library are all fine. Taking on a bunch of little things that you can do quickly (and well) will put you in the right mind-set to accomplish things. Then when you come back to that insurmountable problem, it's simply the next task to check off the list.

No more anxiety.

Like a muscle, no matter how in shape, creativity needs periods of rest to recuperate.

Creativity is a muscle. When your creativity is fit, you can enjoy longer periods of productivity. But like a muscle, no matter how in shape, creativity needs periods of rest to recuperate.

During these periods of rest (ideally, before creative exhaustion sets in), I like to exercise tangential muscles. For example, critically deconstructing and re-creating a work I admire. This applies to design, programming, and music. Examining the fit and finish of a finely crafted work can be invigorating and illuminating.

I am a proponent of practicing multiple disciplines. When I find myself stuck on a design problem, I set it aside and tackle a programming or musical task. My brain can still process the design problem in the background, and it frequently draws unexpected inspiration from the various problem-solving approaches utilized by the different disciplines.

When all else fails, I fall back on performing mundane tasks that do not involve any problem solving. Tidying my work area, doing house or yard work, going for a walk or run, reading a book, or playing a familiar video game. Anything to relax the creative muscle that is too tense.

The strategy I use to overcome creative block is similar to the one I use to get inspired: I prepare a bubble bath. I feel the water surrounding me completely. Without effort, I empty my mind. It's then that the ideas may freely recombine and (re)start their flow.

I PREPARE A BUBBLE BATH

I don't consider encountering difficulty in producing an idea to be creative block. I think of working on a project as playing a game of chess or uncovering clues. I know I can create an appropriate solution, and the only way to do so is by working hard at solving the puzzle.

My first big roadblock is not knowing where to begin. I can spend hours concocting grand ideas but not really progress. You have to start by doing something, even when you don't know what to do. A sketchbook is an essential companion for this. The best way to get ideas is to sketch concepts quickly with a pencil, recording everything—especially the horrible ideas.

The second type of obstacle is getting stuck in the middle of a project. Whenever I am waist-deep in a project and find myself not moving forward, I immediately take a break or work on something else. It is amazing how your subconscious works through the problems. Having a lot of projects means you can easily work on something else and refocus. If I hate the job, I allocate small amounts of time to work on it.

Sometimes when I see an employee stuck on a project, I will ask them to toss the file in the trash. This is highly unorthodox, but it works. Occasionally, you need to just allow yourself to start over again. You would be astounded at how quickly you can do something exponentially better in a fraction of the time after starting fresh.

The third block that I have is the "bad day." We all have them. If I wake up and don't feel well because I am getting sick, I will work on tedious projects—things that require a small amount of thought and a bit of effort. These days are actually valuable because I can organize my work and get things done that I would not want to waste time on during creatively productive days.

For me, the key is to stay in a creative state. Recently I took a weeklong vacation and came back to heaps of work, tons of e-mail, a dirty office, and some heavy deadlines. The little projects were easy to complete but the larger ones loomed over me like dark, intimidating clouds. It made me wonder if this particular block had to do with fear of some kind. After sorting out as many extraneous issues as I could, the ideas started flowing again and I was able to work in peace. Sometimes a block may not even be caused by the project you are working on but by external pressures inhibiting your creativity. I work best when I can relax a little and enjoy what I am working on.

The best thing you can do is pay attention to your workflow and see where you get hung up and make amendments. I hope one of these ideas can help.

TOSS THE FILE IN THE TRASH

de·fine
[dih-fahyn]
What the problem is.

Understanding. I try to understand and define what the problem is. Is it a real or perceived interference? I find, more often than not, it comes from an internal tension rather than a "block" or lack of inspiration. This tension is derived from an opposition between two ideals—normally along the lines of archetype versus unique visual, or personal/emotional investment versus finance. When you can identify what lies behind a strangle on decision making, it makes it a lot easier to reassess what you need or want to achieve with a piece of work and to move forward.

Make all the mistakes necessary to get the resolution. I asked a copywriter once how he overcame writer's block. His advice was to just keep writing, even if it was gibberish. If you can keep pace with your production of ideas, then you can go back and edit it down to something more meaningful. This is an effective way of completing something that you are struggling with or even as a way of starting. It can produce a lot that you can reference during other stages of the project if a solution doesn't work out.

Don't try to "think outside the box." I hate this phrase. To do this you have to imagine a box to think outside of. To imagine your way out of something you have created is an example of the tensions I mentioned earlier. Forcing yourself to be "more creative" is a strange concept because creativity is subjective in nature.

Sitting and waiting for something to happen only makes things worse.

When I am stuck on an idea or in a stage of the design process, movement is the best way out. To swing onto my bike or to just walk down the streets of Berlin or into a park with my dog helps me dissolve the big cluster stuck in my brain. As I experience the movement from point A to B, I feel the pressure to achieve something dissipate. Sitting and waiting for something to happen only makes things worse. Movement loosens my muscles and, hopefully, also my brain and creativity.

Overcoming Creative Block in Ten Easy Steps

1. **Get enough sleep!** Sleep is the best (and easiest) creative aphrodisiac.
2. **Read as much as you can, particularly classics.** If a master of words can't inspire you, see number 3.
3. **Color code your library.** This is fun, and you will realize how many great books you have that you haven't read yet.
4. **More sleep!** You can never get enough.
5. **Force yourself to procrastinate.** Works every time!
6. **Look at the work of Tibor Kalman, Marian Bantjes, Jessica Hische, Christoph Niemann, and Paul Sahre.**
7. **Weep.** And then weep some more.
8. **Surf the Web.** Write inane tweets. Check out your high school friends on Facebook. Feel smug.
9. **Watch *Law & Order: SVU* marathons.** Revel in the ferocious beauty of Olivia Benson.
10. **Remember how L-U-C-K-Y you are to be a creative person to begin with and quit your bellyaching.** Get to work now!

TRAVEL A LOT

For me, taking time away from my working environment is essential to letting my creative juices flow. I have been lucky enough to travel a lot and work in many different cities and encounter various cultures. That is where a lot of my inspiration comes from. Your experiences, the places you see, the people you meet, and the discussions you have will always stay with you and can inspire you at any given moment.

Another source of inspiration when I get stuck in a rut is talking through ideas with my coworkers and friends. This tends to spark something interesting, which is usually worth exploring further. In my experience, the greatest ideas come from a collective approach, so be sure to keep a sketchbook handy. And, if in doubt, talk to people.

I tend to say yes to more than I can do, and the fear of failure keeps the work flowing.

I rely on a few tactics to keep my creativity flowing.

I try to alternate the tenor of my years, like crop rotations. During even-numbered years, I try to do more work and make more of a profit; during odd-numbered years, I travel more and concentrate on personal projects. In 2005 I spent five weeks traveling with an around-the-world ticket, and in 2007 I went to China, Tibet, and Nepal for three weeks. After both trips, I returned to my desk filled with thoughts and initiative to create.

My other strategy is to keep my plate as full as possible. I tend to say yes to more than I can do, and the fear of failure keeps the work flowing.

When I'm really at a loss—when it feels like my designs are simply circling the drain—I will leave the office. There's no point in trying to blindly bump into a solution, so whether it's sketching in the park or reading a book, I avoid trying to use brute force—it's like trying to get rid of the hiccups.

I don't find that creative block happens very often on client projects. The times when I find myself paralyzed are more often on personal projects or open-ended projects where a client allows me to do whatever I want. In these situations the best thing to do is to establish some artificial constraints as quickly as possible.

The constraints of a project are the things that help me be creative. They give me a place to start and often something to rebel against. Identifying a problem or deliverable that I need to address is always the first step. This usually provides sufficient information to set parameters.

Once I have this basic information, I usually find it pretty easy to start generating ideas. Of course, each project is unique and requires a different approach, but I don't do anything revolutionary each time. I tend to make a lot of lists of words that relate to the project. Sometimes I even make a list of words that are the opposite of what I'm trying to communicate. I also make a lot of what I call component sketches. These are essentially visual lists of doodles that relate to the topic. These are especially helpful in looking for interesting ways to combine multiple visuals to create a new meaning. I do this a lot for logo/poster/illustration projects. I also have an extensive library of images that I cull from to build project mood boards. They are useful starting places to decide the look and feel. While mood boards don't always work, they can be incredibly useful and save a lot of time with some of the more sophisticated clients.

If I find myself seriously stuck and unable to focus on a project, I tend to just avoid it for a while and let my subconscious think it over. I find a bike ride or a walk can help me relax and think. Sometimes just a change of location—a different part of the office or a coffee shop—is helpful. Getting a fresh perspective is good. Forcing yourself to articulate the problem to someone else can help to refine the story. If you can successfully explain it to someone else, you're probably onto something.

In the end, a deadline is always the best cure for creative block. Some projects just don't get solved until your survival mechanisms kick in. I sometimes artificially induce this feeling of panic on longer projects by making public commitments to people about presenting work on a particular day. It works reasonably well.

A DEADLINE IS ALWAYS THE BEST CURE

When you're in a creative rut, the most important thing is to get a fresh perspective. Going for a walk or doing the dishes often helps my mind relax, wander, and eventually generate the good ideas I'm looking for. If that doesn't work, or if I don't have time to leave the studio, then I try one of these:

PRETEND
YOU'RE AN
OPOSSUM

☐ **Multiply.** Instead of coming up with one ideal solution, come up with twenty. That way you're not obsessively trying to find the perfect solution. When you have to come up with twenty, you're forced to remove all your filters and let all the ideas come out.

☐ **Shorten the deadline.** You have five days to complete your screenplay/logo/artwork/whatever. Give yourself ten minutes. GO. You'd be surprised how quickly you can come up with something when you're under the gun.

☐ **Step away from the goddamn Internet.** That's right, put away the laptop, the tablet, the smartphone. Access to too much information and too many digital tools and resources can take you off track too easily. Which brings me to…

☐ **Change your materials.** Try pen and paper. It forces you to focus on the basics, on simple solutions. Use crayons. Use chalk. Write on your hand. Take that paper cup from the coffee shop, cut it open, lay it out flat and draw on that. Attack it like a wild animal.

☐ **Pretend.** Stop thinking like a designer or writer or whatever you are for a minute. Pretend you're a pastry chef. Pretend you're an elevator repair contractor. A pilot. A hot dog vendor. How do these people look at the world? Many of these suggestions sound like nonsense. The point is to snap out of your current state and get a fresh perspective. If you need to stand on your head and pretend you're an opossum for a couple of minutes in order to come up with a killer idea/solution/genius work of art, then so be it. Brilliance is inside all of us. We just need to find a way to shake it out.

My inspirations usually come from history.

What works best for me is just powering through: I keep taking pictures until something inspires me. Half of the time, when I go into a project inspired and with a clear goal in mind, what I end up with is completely different anyway.

That said, my inspirations usually come from history. Whether it's the distant past, say, Greek or Roman mythology or Shakespeare, or something much more recent, like the Atomic Age, there's a vast amount of great imagery that's just begging to be taken and turned into something fresh and new.

SOLUTION

Start another project.
Something that is smaller
in scale, different in subject,
and different in medium.

SOLUTION

Drop everything and do
laundry. For some reason,
sitting in front of the washing
machine with nothing else to
do seems to clear my thoughts.

I'm guessing that in nine out of ten cases the so-called writer's block, like a ghost in your own life, simply isn't one—it's just a commonly (mis)used term to cover up depression. Most artists will have little or nothing to say that would reveal what actually causes them to create, what inspires them essentially. It either happens—or it doesn't.

Sure, we can narrow things down a bit—we know which situations, which environments are more likely to create circumstances within which an artist feels an urge to work. Though what *really* motivates us to make music, write texts, take photos, etc.? The inspiration for that for which there is no straightforward, practical need remains a mystery. However, we do know what's stopping us: economic pressure, people who disappoint us, friends that let us down—anything that makes our lives less worth living—occasionally to a point that sadness disables us from *allowing creativity to happen*.

Writer's block can thus be a convenient excuse—to a certain extent it even glamorizes a fairly banal phenomenon that most people will deal with at certain times in their lives. It's certainly not anything that's exclusive to artists. What has changed, however, is the amount of benefit and comfort writer's block can provide to the artist. We live within an economic climate that has destroyed the last vestige of the old-fashioned, romantic ideal of a creative identity; not even an excuse as elusive as the writer's block can expect to be met with much empathy or compassion.

Today increasingly merciless capitalist competition demands that an artist be primarily an entrepreneur. The days when sensitive individuals could hide behind writer's block, a lack of inspiration, and other emotional explanations for their failure to deliver or their inability to function are long gone. Admittedly, great art has very rarely been the work of fully functional, perfectly integrated people, and while it makes little sense to bemoan the good old days, we must be aware that a society that increasingly exposes the arts to such brutal selection under the primacy of economics will pay the high price of cultural decline.

(Special thanks to Lauren Digulio for advice.)

An action is usually prescribed for combating creative block, but I find approaching it with a mind-set more useful. Normally a block appears when you have the intention of achieving something worthwhile and appealing. This is why struggling can be seen as a good thing, and this mind-set will ensure we push through a block instead of accepting uninspired and unappealing work. A triumphant mind-set is one that considers the importance art plays in humanoid territory.

*WE
CAN BE*

*DEEPLY
AFFECTED*

*BY WHAT'S
OUTSIDE*

*OUR
WINDOW*

As members of the human race, we can be deeply affected by what's outside our window. We try to prepare by looking outside and considering which armor to wield against drab weather. It's raining outside. The waterproof cagoule I drape over me is driving the harsh winds aside with its silky streamlined exterior. The sleeves are crimpled at the ends—not liking the way it feels but relishing in its function, I let it aid my poised stance at the foot of a lofty hill. I catch the eyes of many keen, sensible hikers and, perhaps, a few Impressionist painters.

The Impressionists didn't stay inside to paint gods and goddesses. They revolutionized art by taking their canvases outside and celebrating real scenes of people having fun. I stay inside my room alone and paint what I wish I could see outside. For now we try to hike outside, but it is not long before we traipse through today's familiar interior, among rows and racks of products shrieking with their loud parading front covers and phony packaging. The cagoule doesn't brush these loud, shrieking attacks aside like the earlier wind. I'm ill prepared for this scenery.

This is where something I heard Stephen Fry say becomes relevant:

> All of nature is unconditionally and absolutely beautiful wherever it is....The only ugly things you'll ever see when you look out the window are things made by man. If from your earliest age of looking at the world you see yourself as a member of a species who can only uglify and despoil the world, it gives you what psychiatrists would call a deep sense of guilt and guilt as anyone knows is the major cause of aggression…you feel worthless if you don't believe you're part of a species that's actually capable of creating beautiful things, which we are. (BBC, *Room 101*, 2001) ⟶

This is the mind-set. It may come across with wafts of smug and smarm, but please feel no qualms, as it is a trick up the crimpled sleeve of my waterproof jacket to defeat creative blocks. Films, theater, music, literature, design, illustration, and architecture surround us no matter where we live. Every successful person of these trades surely suffers from creative block, but they'll take comfort in knowing they are trying their hardest to create something appealing to the humanoid race. So go forth—it will be worth losing the sleep. But let me tell you this: don't create a dog's dinner of it. A dog's dinner is not pleasing to my keen eye.

The most serious and fulfilling work involves some sort of limit one must come up against.

The concept of an inspirational rut has always presented itself as an issue of confidence, discipline, and even philosophy as opposed to a general lack of direction. In my experience, the most serious and fulfilling work involves some sort of limit(s) one must come up against and overcome. The ability to push through an apparent impasse is almost entirely dependent on the maker's approach to the work, a belief that coming away with something better or worse is a real possibility. I find it difficult to imagine a person working through a serious aesthetic problem without such an outlook, although it is not impossible to stumble upon solutions without it. While mistaking ends for limits is a necessary side effect of this process, the hardship endured clearly pales in comparison with the gains made.

I've tried many things whenever I find myself in a creative slump, when it feels like I'm just pushing things around aimlessly hoping something will stick and show me the way out. I force myself to keep trying, tell myself that the answer is just around the corner, and any second now (and multiple design files later) I'll be wondering why that was so difficult.

The solution is obvious!

Sometimes this "just push through it" approach works. Often, though, it doesn't, and I waste valuable time. The thing I found works best for me is to push it aside and go do something completely different. Hop on my bike for a spin through the local marshes, do the grocery shopping, read comics, or even watch TV. (I have discovered through rigorous testing that watching shopping channels is excellent for this.) Mundane things that take away my focus from the work but allow me to wander off in thought and let things just happen. Distraction is actually a good thing, and I'll often think of a solution when I'm not behind a desk, which is why I always carry a notepad and pen with me—just in case.

Actually, sitting here writing this "strategy" document, my mind is wandering, and I'm sitting here thinking, "What else can I say that hasn't been said before or that doesn't sound like the most obvious thing in the world?!" And the thing is, I can't—because I don't believe there is a set rule or system to overcome a creative block. I need to be able to let my mind wander, see things, and then mentally reconnect the dots that eventually lead to an answer in an organic way.

The best ideas happen when you're not trying to come up with one.

WATCH TV

(I HAVE DISCOVERED THROUGH RIGOROUS TESTING THAT WATCHING SHOPPING CHANNELS IS EXCELLENT FOR THIS.)

Everything isn't a joke, but it's all pretty funny.

Sometimes being a graphic designer is as simple as following directions. We are commissioned for a job, are briefed, and agree on a price. We roll up our sleeves, we open the factory, and, as smoke belches from our Wacom pens, we complete the work and are paid. Commerce! It fulfills a part of our brain that likes to solve problems and complete tasks. Anyone who tells you there is no value in this sort of thing is a liar or a teenager (full disclosure: I am scared of both). And if this all sounds too mechanical and dull, let me remind you that there is more. Much more. There is a whole different part of our brain that we get paid to use: the creative part. It's much more glamorous and fun, but as you might expect, a lot more difficult to control. The good news is that creative block is all in your head. Unfortunately, so are all the good ideas.

So how then do we get to all these good ideas? Graphic design is a funny profession in that the amount of hours logged doesn't always equate to better work. Design is not just assembly line (although some people think it is), and we are well served to not treat it like one. There seems to be a much more complex algorithm used when determining one's own personal formula for successful creative endeavors, and a lot of the things involved have nothing to do with graphic design.

There is a Woody Guthrie quote that has been rattling around my head for some time now: "Take it easy, but take it." I think that sums up a large part of my work ethic, how I tackle creative blocks, and how I (try to) live my life. You need to show up, follow through, and work hard. That is a given. But I really believe if you want to tap into this deeper part of your brain and make some unexpected connections (where the good ideas come from), you have to work just as hard on having a life outside of your day job. This can mean different things for different people. I have been finding a lot of creative inspiration and excitement in some things that were very important to me as a teenager. Outdated mantras and classic rock lyrics and things like that. Basic stuff that my snarky early twenties almost killed. It's kind of silly, but taking yourself too seriously only gets in the way of creative thinking. Everything isn't a joke, but it's all pretty funny.

I just start working.
Then I work as long as I have something decent done.
Then I take a break and usually start all over again.
Usually it works. And if not, I take a longer break and try again.
Good music is also needed.
Just a lot of work. No miracles.

JUST A LOT OF WORK. <u>NO MIRACLES.</u>

I pick a record. A good one. One that makes me bounce. One that makes me laugh. One that makes me cry. I listen to it, hear it, simply feel it. I let my moods take me on a journey. I let inspiration come along. I always listen to music while working. Silence kills the mood.

I dive directly into action. I avoid a clean table. I avoid an empty canvas. I might pick something I created earlier. Something good. Something I am proud of. I place it on a canvas and take it further. I develop it and play around with it. I leave it and introduce myself to a doodle I have just met on the corner of the paper by accident.

I make myself feel uncomfortable. I congratulate myself. Not too often. I stay humble and work hard.

You've been working hard all year and then suddenly your dream project lands on your lap—a once-in-a-lifetime chance, a real career maker. Sitting down at your desk with your trusty pen and paper ready to do battle and that's when it hits you. Nothing, absolutely nothing but tumbleweeds rolling through your mind. Try as you might, you just can't get the creative juices flowing. Why? Yesterday you were an overflowing ideas fountain!

TAKE A

BIG STEP

BACK

Everyone experiences this at some point or another—normally when you least expect it or, better still, when it's the least convenient—but it's how we overcome it that makes us who we are. As with most things, there is no universal technique to beat this condition (and believe me, it is a condition), but I can tell you what I do to try to beat it, hopefully arming you with the right tools in case you too are in the same predicament.

If I have a bit of time and am not up against a deadline (a rarity), I like to take a big step back. If I try to force out an idea, my brain seems to just go around in circles and trip over itself, resulting in an idea of low quality. By taking my mind off the task at hand, it's almost like I'm tricking my gray matter into resetting itself. Stepping outside of the studio, taking in the surrounding sights, sounds, and fresh air. Okay, maybe not so much the fresh-air part—I am in central London after all—but you get the gist.

But what if you have to get something over to your client within a couple of hours? The principle is the same. I know it's painfully obvious almost to the point of a cliché, but being away from the neon glare of monitors and flicking through a book or magazine helps me click into gear. The simple act of thumbing through a book lets you pick up new directions and routes for the strangest of reasons. I might be reading through a completely unrelated article and suddenly a word jumps out of the page and hits me, sparking a chain reaction. I love those moments—those Archimedes's eureka moments. It's what makes doing what we do worthwhile. It's your very own personal classic underdog tale—going from down and out to winning the title (or, more likely, a pitch). It's almost as if creative block is a necessary evil of the creative process.

They say variety is the spice of life. Increasing my palette helped me grow in many areas as a designer and in many ways decreased my chances of having designer's block.

I used to design primarily for the Web; I would get burned out all the time. It's like eating the same food for every meal. Then I started getting into software interface and icon design. It felt so fresh to me—like discovering a new fruit. Not only was it liberating to be using my skill set for a slightly different focus, these new interests also provided fresh ideas and energy for designing for the Web. Being able to tackle design problems in different areas made me a better designer all around.

Another way I battle creative block is by challenging myself creatively in completely different fields. I took on photography as a hobby many years ago. It allowed me to be creative in a totally different way. The same goes for drawing or playing music, painting, etc. Finding success in other creative outlets boosts my confidence, releases stress, and also aids in the creative work that pays the bills.

A change of scenery often helps me get through creative block. Whenever I start a new project where brainstorming and conceptualizing needs to be done, I'll go to a coffee shop to work. Sitting at a coffee shop with just my notebook, laptop, and earbuds has never failed. Something about the atmosphere (and access to unlimited amounts of caffeine) does it for me.

FINDING SUCCESS IN OTHER CREATIVE OUTLETS BOOSTS MY CONFIDENCE

I don't believe in writer's block.

Yes, there may have been days or even weeks at a time when I have not written—even when I may have wanted to—but that doesn't mean I was blocked. It simply means I was in the wrong place at the wrong time. Or, as I'd like to argue, exactly the right place at the right time.

The creative process has more than one kind of expression. There's the part you could show in a movie montage—the furious typing or painting or equation solving where the writer, artist, or mathematician accomplishes the output of the creative task. But then there's also the part that happens invisibly, under the surface. That's when the senses are perceiving the world, the mind and heart are thrown into some sort of dissonance, and the soul chooses to respond.

That response doesn't just come out like vomit after a bad meal. There's no such thing as pure expression. Rather, because we live in a social world with other people whose perceptual apparatus needs to be penetrated with our ideas, we must formulate, strategize, order, and then articulate. It is that last part that is visible as output or progress, but it only represents, at best, 25 percent of the process.

Real creativity transcends time. If you are not producing work, then chances are you have fallen into the infinite space between the ticks of the clock where reality is created. Don't let some capitalist taskmaster tell you otherwise—even if he happens to be in your own head.

AT THE

BEST

☆☆☆☆☆☆☆☆☆☆☆☆

IDEA

☆☆☆☆☆☆☆☆☆☆☆☆

EVER

☆☆☆☆☆☆☆☆☆☆☆☆

Running out of ideas sucks. Sadly, I don't believe there is any way to avoid this unfortunate fate. When my creative well runs dry, I don't subscribe to any meditative step-by-step formula for striking water again. On the contrary, I prefer a self-inflicted method of torture—that is, sitting at the desk all night and day, gnarled pencil in hand, suffering mental and emotional anguish for as many hours as it takes to get through the loads of mud to find a gem. It's an incredibly uncomfortable process, which may even last a couple of days.

I recall one spell, about a year ago, that went on for a whole week. Seven days! I truly didn't think I would make it. This struggle can affect hygiene, sleep habits, eyesight, basic decision-making skills, and maybe even your ability to distinguish good from evil. However, once you get through it and find that incredible flow of genius content you are so used to having, it's pure euphoria— the biggest rush. You win, you've conquered the challenge, this is the BEST IDEA EVER, and…oh wait, they needed two separate proposals?

Here are things I do, in no particular order, to get over creative block:

Part A

- ☐ Go to the movies
- ☐ Go to museums and galleries
- ☐ Watch trashy TV
- ☐ Go shopping
- ☐ Read junky magazines
- ☐ Take a long walk, usually down Fifth Avenue

Part B

- ☐ Clean out my closet
- ☐ Buy cooking supplies or art materials (same thing)
- ☐ Buy new make-up
- ☐ Get a haircut
- ☐ Buy a new pair of shoes or boots

Activities in Part A help me get outside myself, may inspire me, and help me to see and think in a new way. Activities in Part B are all self-improvement projects. When I feel good about myself I am ready for the next thing.

WHEN I FEEL
GOOD
ABOUT MYSELF
I AM READY FOR
THE NEXT THING

For me the fear of failure is everything. It keeps me honest, it motivates me, it makes me research, and it inspires me to try new things. While I'm trying to make sure the project is a success, there are usually a dozen or two creative barriers to overcome. The best way for me to overcome these barriers is by sticking to a set creative process that works for me.

When approaching any project, I tend to follow a basic path: research, concept development, visual development (sketches), and then of course the "real work." I find that if I work within this format in some way or another, I manage to avoid some of the creative block that might occur later, when I sit down to create the real work. In a perfect world, this would always work. But we all know better than that.

When the inevitable creative ruts do occur, I usually just move on to a totally new idea and come back to the tough one later, with a clear mind. A lot of problems work themselves out when I approach the project from a different angle. Then, after rotating through my ideas and approaches a couple of times, I go back and look at all of the ideas (sketches, photos, rationales) again.

I know that a lot of designers and artists like to approach things much more organically, but this is the way I like to work. Starting a project with a set plan and process protects me later from the many frustrations that come with any piece.

For a long time, I tried fighting creative block. At one period of my life, I would take long walks. At another stage, I would watch an episode or two of my favorite TV show before getting back to my desk. (It never really helped, but I liked to believe it did.) My apartment really benefited from the time when I was trying to beat creative ruts by clearing my head through cleaning.

My biggest revelation in terms of overcoming creative block was realizing that my best pieces were the outcomes of my biggest struggles. The ones with which I had spent countless hours staring at a wall or crying about how nothing in this piece made sense. Coming to realize these ruts were actually crucial to performing better and coming up with more innovative and less predictable results completely changed my take on them. Now, when I hit a creative dead end, I overcome it by seeing it as an opportunity to rethink, re-evaluate, and make something great.

MY BEST PIECES WERE THE OUTCOMES OF MY BIGGEST STRUGGLES

Some of my favorite work has happened in the delusional, desperate hours of late nights.

When I was first approached about this topic, I debated whether or not I ought to participate. I feared that by refusing to take part, I'd be cursed with a lifetime of creative stumps. Inversely, by accepting, I'd have to consciously consider a topic I am a bit frightened to explore. Clearly, I am damned either way, but I've chosen to write.

My own fears and misgivings feed this superstition—not that I believe in black cats or broken mirrors. Discussing creative block legitimizes it, and I'd prefer to change topics and relax a bit.

To start—I'm going to distill and introduce the three types of creatives. First up, the absolutely confident artist—disregard them, they didn't buy this book, because they never suffer from creative stumps and often spend their time creating mediocre works of inflated importance. Second, the scared-stiff artist—this type of creative has forgotten we only live once, and if you meet one, please remind them. Third, the happy-medium artist—thankfully, these are the most common artists and the folks who worry about what they create. They mean well, bare their souls, and occasionally produce beautiful works of staggeringly complex, conflicted beauty. The third artist fails and overcomes, and this struggle leads to honest work made with love.

When I'm feeling superstitious, I find it's best to embrace it and take breaks. I've learned to leverage procrastination and to love deadlines. I'll sometimes sit on my hands, because deadlines are stimulants, and some of my favorite work has definitely happened in the delusional, desperate hours of late nights.

I've also learned to finish things I start—love it or hate it. There is no better lesson than those taught through failure, and no better fuel than the insistence on overcoming it. For me, following through is a success in itself, even if the finished work is just a lesson.

And lastly, I look around for inspiration. I'll watch films, read books, walk to the gallery—things that remind me that it's all more or less been done and in all likelihood better than I can hope to do it myself. I have to be comfortable with adapting and decorating the wheel, because it's only on occasion one will have the opportunity to reinvent it.

Post-production and visual effects is often a very technical world to inhabit. The eternal struggle is to make things looks as real as possible, but when you break things down into layers, pixels, render passes, and so on, they become so far removed from flesh-and-blood reality. Perfectly sharp, glossy—and so not *real*, but *really constructed*.

This is when the need to get creative kicks in. Instead of layering A over B and saying, "Hey, presto! We're done!" you really have to think what can be done to make your brain and eye believe what they are seeing. I've spent hours looking at something wondering why it doesn't look quite right. This is the block that I struggle with.

There are certain paths we need to follow in order for everything to technically work, but there are no hard-and-fast rules otherwise. In my opinion, if something works and looks good—job done. Although I'm no fan of the phrase "thinking outside the box," this is key to getting past that block.

Instead of looking at what you have and what's wrong with it (or why it doesn't look right), try to find what does work and what you can make work. If you have to, pull every image and every part of the image to bits, then put it together again with the bits you like. Use every trick and every button in front of you. Don't feel like you have to use things as they were intended to be used.

Also, don't be lazy. If you feel like a shot or a scene is missing that little bit of reality, go get it. Take a small part from here, another part from there, and, just for kicks, something totally random from somewhere else. This is how my mentors and talented coworkers continue to astound me. You never know. That little added detail may just be that piece of reality you need.

USE EVERY TRICK & EVERY BUTTON IN FRONT of YOU

Casual drawing in public usually shakes something loose.

We started our little design garage band as two freelancers working from home studios. And just like any good freelancer, we spent a lot time ass-shining the seats of our favorite coffee shops. Despite now having an office with employees and interns, our go-to method for breaking the spell of creative block hasn't changed much at all. We need to limit the distractions in the studio and get back to pure drawing. Our sketchbooks are where most of our ideas begin, so we keep them around all the time—new ones as well as old. We'll leave the office for a cappuccino and a few hours of doodling, and then reconvene to critique and review sketches and notes. We've always found that the one huge benefit of having a collaborative partner is that dialogue about ideas. Before long, the other person's suggestion or criticism transforms a seed of a sketch into an exciting idea that wasn't immediately visible to the individual. Maybe it's the distance from office phone calls and e-mails, the comforting white noise of café chatter, or just the caffeine, but casual drawing in public usually shakes something loose. And should the coffee-shop remedy fail, we're likely to abandon the pens and the pencils altogether and make a beeline for the earliest matinee showing.

Nothing clears the head in an instant or makes a grown man cry like spicy food. My personal recommendations are Tom Yum Goong (a Thai sour and spicy clear-broth soup, usually cooked with seafood or chicken), Pepper Crabs (the legendary Singaporean dish— the burn is so good, even your fingers hurt), and Curry Fish Head (often cooked with a generous amount of vegetables, like okra and eggplants, and great paired with a bowl of rice).

When you're done with the tears and the sweating, everything seems insignificant compared to what you've just endured.

EAT
SPICY FOOD

In a moment of mild exasperation, a frequent collaborator of ours remarked that our motto ought to be, "Why do it twice when you can do it thrice?" In some ways, this phrase might come as close as possible to encapsulating our working method and approach: the strongly held belief that the labor of design is, at its core, about more than glib inspirations and momentary insights. Rather, the best design is about hard work, considering problems deeply, iteratively pushing solutions further, and creating things with the utmost craft until they seem to burst with invested meaning and visual refinement. Sometimes those same solutions, having been so thoroughly investigated, can shed the weight of the multiple meanings they may have accrued and become light in their touch, returning to a purer state but nonetheless transformed through their many rounds, versions, and stages. Designs that seem simple yet resonate vibrantly often do so because they are not the first solutions: instead they are just the most recent stop on a long and thorough course of exploration.

Whenever someone claims to have a foolproof, patented methodology for making great design, we are skeptical: in our experience, design happens mostly through long discussion, constant inquiry, ongoing experimentation, formal rigor, periodic happenstance, a deadline, and many long nights. Seen this way, the actual products of design fade to the background, giving way to the way things are made and the focused passion that goes into them. Perhaps the corollary to our unofficial motto from earlier would be this famous line by Samuel Beckett: "Try again. Fail again. Fail better."

Everything can be flipped in a way that can be more pleasant and fun. The challenge is about finding that fun factor in each project. I believe that when you're working on something you like and trying to keep that feeling until the end of the process, you will have good results.

EVERYTHING

CAN BE

FLIPPED

Find inspiration through random occurrences during the course of a day.

I don't follow an exact formula that tells me where or how I will find inspiration. I seem to find inspiration through random occurrences during the course of a day. While there are moments when I really need some eye candy to get my visual brain working, I usually try not to look at blogs that are solely devoted to graphic design, as I always strive to create work that speaks my own visual language.

When I first started practicing graphic design, I had the bad habit of trying to emulate my heroes: tDR, Build, Müller-Brockmann, Wim Crouwel, and Otl Aicher. Now I'm lucky enough to have a style that feels like my own (a blend of the modernist tendencies I love so much with a subtle humanist touch). Since I have a style of my own, I only worry about the ideas rather than the aesthetic, as I usually have a rough idea of how the final outcome could look.

Whenever I need inspiration, I go for walks and try to find interesting things around me. I always carry a camera with me to document these moments. Inspiration, for me, is twofold: as a designer I observe people dealing with things, visually or in their behavior; as an artist I look for good composition and interesting moments that almost tell a story without words.

My most serious bout of creative block happened between 2008 and 2009. I had just finished several years of shooting fun, lucrative editorial and commercial projects, but when I looked through my work, none of the images were totally mine. My portfolio had become full of other people's concepts. I felt I had become a glorified technician, executing ideas that I didn't own. They didn't express anything personal or reflect my most deeply held sensibilities. And worse than that, I had become accustomed to big productions, relying on many people and moving parts. I thought everything had to be complicated and "the best ever."

This was frustrating and stifling, and I became afraid of failure. I also became afraid to trust myself, my instincts, my own ideas.

So I stripped everything away and started over: no crews, stylists, or hired talent—just me and a camera. I stopped going into the studio every day because inspiration does not strike in studios. I had to go out, be with people, try new things, be observant and a good listener. And eventually, I was inspired: people are amazing and have an infinite number of stories waiting to be told.

I started shooting personal projects—projects that were close to me. And after time, I rediscovered my voice and personal vision. I shot things that I found entertaining, unusual, or intriguing, and I didn't worry about what I would do with the images. I only concerned myself with capturing that which had drawn me to the story in the first place.

Now 90 percent of my portfolio is a result of this approach. This has opened new doors in the fine art, editorial, and commercial markets. The work feels more honest, emotional, and real. The work feels like me.

INSPIRATION
DOES NOT STRIKE
IN STUDIOS.

ROCK A

ID ROLL

Thanks to my wonderful mom and dad. While not directly involved in the creation of this collection of words and pages, I generally attribute any and every wonderful occurrence in this world to them, so they must be mentioned!

Thanks to my incredible sister, Holly Cornell. She is a most excellent sister. Both wise and talented, she is currently powering the majority of New York City with her magical energy.

I am very grateful to my inimitable cousin Sara Murray. We spent many a long hour staring at computer screens together, constructing the foundations of the book in between periodic ice cream breaks.

My personal creative upbringing is indebted to Scott Hansen. I couldn't ask for a better friend and mentor.

Thanks to my friends Blake Byers and Chad Byers, Michael Chang, Phil Mills, Will Pringle, and Nikki Desuasido. I am forever grateful for their feedback, support, and love.

Many loud and boisterous thanks to Sara Bader at Princeton Architectural Press. It was her vision that took this idea from the Internet to the pages of this book. Her guidance and encouragement in the early stages of this project were invaluable.

I am also very grateful to Linda Lee, for her continued support and assistance in the latter stages of this project. What fun it was to see it all come together.

Thanks to Erik Spiekermann for his splendid foreword and a wonderful afternoon spent discussing our favorite numbers and the innumerable benefits of Gibson guitars.

Finally, thanks to all of the inspiring creative people who generously contributed to this book. This resource would be impossible without them. I think it's worth noting that all of them weathered an enormous number of correspondences from me, which is an admirable feat in itself. The e-mails will stop now. I promise.

Robert Andersen is a product designer and creative lead at Square. He was formerly a product designer at Apple. *implodr.tumblr.com*

Chuck Anderson is an artist based in Grand Rapids, Michigan. His design studio is NoPattern. *nopattern.com*

Curtis Baigent is an art director and motion-and-design artist from Wellington, New Zealand, who currently wanders the world in search of something he cannot yet put his finger on. *curtisbaigent.com*

Tom Balchin is a British graphic designer. *tombalchin.co.uk*

Ben Barry is a communication designer, illustrator, printer, and thinker at Facebook. *designforfun.com*

Jonathan Bartlett is a New York City–based illustrator. *seejbdraw.com*

Kyle Bean is an artist and designer based in Brighton, England. He specializes in handmade models, sets, and props. *kylebean.co.uk*

Dan Blackman is a graphic designer and art director currently living and working in the Philadelphia area. *dblackman.com*

Wilson Brown is creative director at Antfood and is based in Brooklyn. *antfood.com*

Dan Cassaro is a freelance designer, animator, and printmaker living and working in Brooklyn. He puts words on paper so that they might be accountable for themselves. He is taking it easy, but still taking it. *youngjerks.com*

Catalogtree is a Dutch graphic design studio based in Arnhem, the Netherlands. *catalogtree.net*

Michael Cina is a graphic designer and creative director at Cina Associates. *michaelcinaassociates.com*

Nancy Sharon Collins is the principle of Collins, LLC, and director of special projects for AIGA New Orleans. *nancysharoncollinsstationer.com*

Jon Contino is a Brooklyn-based illustrator and creative director at CXXVI Clothing Co. *joncontino.com*

Andy Cruz is the art director at House Industries. *houseind.com/about/housebios/andy*

Sara Cwynar is a New York City–based artist and graphic designer. *saracwynar.com*

Claire Dederer is a longtime contributor to the *New York Times*. Her articles have also appeared in *Vogue, Real Simple, The Nation, New York*, and *Yoga Journal*, on Slate and Salon, and in newspapers across the country. *clairedederer.com*

Jax De León is a Brooklyn-based graphic designer. *jaxdeleon.com*

Daniel Dennett, the author of *Breaking the Spell* (2006), *Freedom Evolves* (2003), and *Darwin's Dangerous Idea* (1995), is a professor and codirector of the Center for Cognitive Studies at Tufts University. *ase.tufts.edu/cogstud/incbios/dennettd/dennettd.htm*

Deru is Benjamin Wynn, an electronic-music producer residing in Los Angeles. *deru.la*

Thomas Doyle is an artist living and working in New York City. *thomasdoyle.net*

Aaron Duffy is the creative director at 1st Ave Machine and Special Guest. He resides in Brooklyn. *aaronduffy.com*

eBoy is Kai Vermehr, Steffen Sauerteig, and Svend Smital. The studio creates reusable pixel objects and adapts them to build complex and extensible artwork. *hello.eboy.com/eboy*

Michael Erard is a journalist who writes about language, mostly. He is a contributing writer for Design Observer and the author of the forthcoming *Babel No More: The Search for the World's Most Extraordinary Language Learners* (2012). *michaelerard.com*

Experimental Jetset is a small, independent graphic design studio based in Amsterdam. Its three members are Marieke Stolk, Danny van den Dungen, and Erwin Brinkers. *experimentaljetset.nl*

Aaron Feaver is a photographer based in Los Angeles. *feaverishphotography.com*

Nicolas Felton is the cofounder of Daytum.com and a member of the product design team at Facebook. *feltron.com*

Sean Freeman is an illustrator based in London. *thereis.co.uk*

Urs Furrer is a visual-effects artist based in Brisbane, Australia. *ursafurrer.com*

Jasper Goodall is an artist who works as a freelance illustrator. He also teaches an illustration-degree course at the University of Brighton in the United Kingdom. *jaspergoodall.com*

Superfamous is the Los Angeles–based studio of Dutch interaction designer **Folkert Gorter**. It focuses primarily on content-driven networks, creative communities, and visual publishing interfaces. *cargo.superfamous.com*

Kalle Gustafsson is a Swedish photographer. *kallegustafsson.com*

Jessica Hagy is a writer based in Seattle. She is the creator of the "Indexed" project. *thisisindexed.com*

Scott Hansen is a San Francisco–based musician (Tycho) and designer (ISO50). *blog.iso50.com*

Christian Helms is the owner of Helms Workshop, an award-winning design and brand-development studio. *helmsworkshop.com*

J. C. Herz is the author of *Joystick Nation: How Videogames Ate Our Quarters, Won Our Hearts, and Rewired Our Minds* (1997) and *Surfing on the Internet* (1995).

Todd Hido is an American artist and photographer. He is currently based in San Francisco. *toddhido.com*

Kim Holm currently works as a director, designer, and motion-graphics artist in Oslo. *kimholm.com*

Kim Høltermand is a freelance architecture and landscape photographer from Kirke-Værløse, Copenhagen. *holtermand.dk*

Mario Hugo is a New York City–based artist, graphic designer, and illustrator. He is cofounder of the creative management agency Hugo and Marie. *mariohugo.com*

Sarah Illenberger is an artist living in Berlin. *sarahillenberger.com/index.html*

Shaun Inman is a designer, developer, and composer who believes that occasionally talking about yourself in the third person is an acceptable, necessary evil. *shauninman.com/pilation*

Mark Jardine is an interaction designer based in San Jose, California. He is also an illustrator, photographer, car enthusiast, and designer for Tapbots. *markjardine.com*

Inka Järvinen is a Helsinki-based graphic designer and illustrator. *inkajarvinen.com*

The drawings of illustrator **Marc Johns** have been exhibited in New York City, San Francisco, Los Angeles, Vancouver, Athens, and elsewhere. *marcjohns.com*

Dan Kenneally is an art director by day and a visual artist by night. *dankenneally.com*

Aaron Koblin is an artist specializing in data and digital technologies. *aaronkoblin.com*

Alexandra Lange is a critic, journalist, and architectural historian based in Brooklyn. She teaches architecture criticism in the D-Crit Program at the School of Visual Arts in New York City and the Urban Design and Architecture Studies program at New York University. *observersroom.designobserver.com/alexandralange*

Ji Lee, born in South Korea and raised in Brazil, was formerly the creative director at Google. He is currently the creative director at Facebook and lives in Palo Alto, California. *pleaseenjoy.com*

Jamie Lidell is an English musician and soul singer living in New York City. *jamielidell.com*

Matthew Lyons is a British illustrator. *matthew-lyons.com*

Paul Madonna is a San Francisco–based illustrator and cartoonist. *paulmadonna.com*

Mike McQuade is a graphic designer and illustrator based in Chicago. *mikemcquade.com*

Debbie Millman is a writer, educator, artist, brand consultant, and host of the radio show Design Matters. *debbiemillman.com*

Michael Milosh, known professionally as **Milosh**, is a Canadian electronic musician. *myspace.com/milosh*

Cameron Moll is a designer and author living in Sarasota, Florida. He is the founder of Authentic Jobs, among other endeavors. *cameronmoll.com*

Belgian design director **Tom Muller** specializes in graphic design, typography, identity design, and illustration. *hellomuller.com*

Jason Munn is a graphic designer based in Oakland, California. *jasonmunn.com/posters.php*

Musician **Alexi Murdoch** was born in London and attended college in North Carolina. He currently splits his time between New York City and a small house on the remote west coast of Scotland, where he spends his days writing and working on a small wooden sailing boat. *aleximurdoch.com*

Tim Navis is a photographer living in Los Angeles. *navisphotography.com*

Network Osaka is the design studio of Derek Kim. *networkosaka.com*

Felix Ng is the founder and art director of Silnt. *work.felixng.com*

Nice Collective is a San Francisco–based menswear label. *nicecollective.com*

Christoph Niemann is an illustrator, designer, and author of "Abstract Sunday," a column for the *New York Times Magazine*. *christophniemann.com*

Lotta Nieminen is a multidisciplinary designer and illustrator from Helsinki. *lottanieminen.com/index.html*

Simon C. Page is a designer based in London. *simoncpage.co.uk/blog*

John Passafiume is a Brooklyn-based designer and illustrator specializing in hand lettering and formal aesthetics. *johnpassafiume.com*

Michael C. Place is the creative director at Build, a London-based graphic design consultancy. *wearebuild.com*

Sam Potts is a graphic designer based in New York City. *sampottsinc.com*

Project Projects is a design studio focusing on print, identity, exhibition, and interactive work with clients in art and architecture. The studio was founded in 2004 by Prem Krishnamurthy and Adam Michaels; Rob Giampietro joined as a principal in 2010. *projectprojects.com*

Jesse Rieser is a photographer based in Los Angeles. *jesserieser.com*

Pete Rossi is a Scottish graphic designer. *pgerossi.co.uk*

Camm Rowland is an executive creative director at Digital Kitchen, a creative agency. *cammrowland.com*

Douglas Rushkoff is an author, teacher, and documentarian. He teaches media studies at New York University and the New School, serves as technology columnist for the Daily Beast, and lectures around the world. *rushkoff.com*

Chaz Russo is a senior designer at *Relevant* magazine. *reckerhouse.com*

Vesa Sammalisto is a Finnish illustrator and graphic designer based in Berlin. *vesa-s.com*

Jon Saunders is a motion designer and director working at Psyop in New York City. *jonsaunders.tv*

Philipp Schaerer is a Swiss artist and architect. *philippschaerer.ch*

Paula Scher is an American graphic designer, illustrator, painter, and art educator. She was the first female principal at Pentagram, which she joined in 1991. *pentagram.com*

Ulrich Schnauss is an electronic musician based in London. *myspace.com/ulrichschnauss*

Christopher Simmons is a designer, writer, educator, and owner of the San Francisco design office MINE. *minesf.com, christopherchsimmons.com*

Erik Spiekermann is a German typographer and designer. *spiekermann.com*

Astrid Stavro is the creative director at Studio Astrid Stavro, based in the Balearic Islands, Spain. *astridstavro.com*

Jason Kernevich and Dustin Summers are **The Heads of State**, a design shop based in Philadelphia. *theheadsofstate.com*

Alex Trochut was born in 1981 in Barcelona. He studied graphic design at ELISAVA (Barcelona School of Design and Engineering) and started working as an illustrator and typographer in 2007. *alextrochut.com*

Tomi Um is a noodle-obsessed illustrator/textile designer/printmaker based in New York City. *tomiillustration.com*

Julien Vallée is a graphic designer, art director, and an artist from Montréal who creates tangible images for clients that range from the *New York Times Magazine* to Swatch and MTV-One. *jvallee.com/index_jvallee.html*

Khoi Vinh was formerly the design director at nytimes.com. He is now the cofounder and CEO of Lascaux, makers of the world's first social collage app, Mixel, for the iPad. *subtraction.com*

James White is an artist, designer, and public speaker. He is also a proud Canadian, spectrum explorer, and the one-man wrecking crew behind Signalnoise Studio. *blog.signalnoise.com*

Blake Whitman is the vice president of creative development at Vimeo. *blakewhitman.tumblr.com*

James Wignall is a director and illustrator based in London. *mutanthands.com*

Published by
Princeton Architectural Press
37 East Seventh Street
New York, New York 10003

Visit our website at www.papress.com

Editors: Linda Lee and Nicola Brower
Designer: Elana Schlenker

Special thanks to:
Bree Anne Apperley, Sara Bader,
Janet Behning, Fannie Bushin,
Megan Carey, Carina Cha, Andrea Chlad,
Russell Fernandez, Will Foster,
Diane Levinson, Jennifer Lippert,
Jacob Moore, Gina Morrow,
Katharine Myers, Margaret Rogalski,
Dan Simon, Andrew Stepanian,
Paul Wagner, and Joseph Weston
of Princeton Architectural Press
—Kevin C. Lippert, publisher

Library of Congress
Cataloging-in-Publication Data
Breakthrough! : 90 proven strategies to
spark your imagination / Alex Cornell ;
with a foreword by Erik Spiekermann. —
First [edition].
    pages   cm
ISBN 978-1-61689-039-1 (pbk. : alk. paper)
1. Artist's block. 2. Creation (Literary,
artistic, etc.)—Miscellanea. I. Cornell,
Alex, 1984- editor of compilation.
N71.B695 2012
701'.15—dc23
                                2012002060